Rabbi
Menachem
Mendel
of Kotzk

Rabbi Menachem Mendel of Kotzk

A Biographical Study of the Chasidic Master

By Dr. Joseph Fox

published by Bash Publications, Inc. New York

RABBI MENACHEM MENDEL
OF KOTZK

FIRST EDITION
First Impression — June 1988

Published by
BASH PUBLICATIONS, INC.

ISBN 0—932351—21—2

Distributed by:
MAZNAIM PUBLISHING CORPORATION
4304 12th Avenue
Brooklyn, New York 11219

Typography by BASH PUBLICATIONS, INC.
Printed in the U.S.A.

This book is dedicated to:

My beloved wife, Bronia בלומה

My daughter, Sheila Shulamith שולמית

My grandchildren:
Karen Ruth Drexler חיה רבקה
Michael Nathan מיכאל נתן
Debra Sue דבורה

My greatgranddaughter:
Jennifer Fox Drexler נחמה

Table of Contents

Introduction

Rabbi Menachem Mendel of Kotzk was one of the most captivating personalities the chasidic movement has produced. In his own eyes he was a tzaddik, an intermediary between a community of faithful disciples and the Supernatural; at the same time, he remained a man of rational thought and critical mind. He was a recognized leader with untold numbers of devout adherents, who flocked to his residence and waited anxiously for every utterance of his lips. Yet he was by nature a recluse. He challenged many of the accepted manners of belief and behavior hallowed by the very same people who admired him. He was a high-spirited man of unusual will-power and daring, whose professed life's mission was to bring a renaissance of chasiduth and restore it to its pristine purity; simultaneously, he was incapable of practical action and torn by unresolved inner conflicts.

The story of the Rabbi of Kotzk inevitably revolves around the events of a particular Sabbath Eve in 1839. On that fateful night, he withdrew in large part from society, choosing to remain secluded for the remaining two decades of his life. One's view of the Kotzker is inextricably bound with his version of what actually transpired on that night, of what Rabbi Menachem Mendel really said. Hence, Rabbi Mordecai Joseph Leiner was so disturbed by the Kotzker's deportment that he went and founded his own branch of chasiduth. On the other hand, Rabbi Isaac Meir of Ger remained at his rebbe's side and fought to discredit the rumors which were being spread concerning the Kotzker.

The story of Rabbi Menachem Mendel of Kotzk brings into focus many of the unresolved problems and conflicting issues that still animate present-day Jewish intellectual life. The events that led to the tragic Friday night of 1839 and the air of mystery that surrounded it are as intriguing and poignant to us as they were to his contemporaries. In the reconstruction and understanding of all the thoughts and deeds that led to the eruption of that historic Friday night rest the only hope for a reasonable solution of the "riddle of Kotzk."

All the hopes and aspirations of the Rabbi of Kotzk, his resolve to revolutionize the chasidic movement and to become "even greater than the Ba'al Shem Tov," the entire meaning of his life — all of these are involved in the events of that memorable Sabbath Eve. And yet, we have no clear accounting of what really happened.

While some among the "enlightened" claim that Rabbi Menachem Mendel approached blasphemy, all the chasidic writers assure us that nothing extraordinary took place, and that all the rumors were a reprehensible vilification of the saintly rabbi's memory. Yet the unusually strong language used in a letter written by the most devoted disciple of Kotzk, Rabbi Isaac Meir of Ger; the fact that so many of the faithful defected from the cause of Kotzk and followed the rebellious Rabbi Mordecai Joseph Leiner of Izbitza; and the ensuing twenty years of Rabbi Menachem Mendel's confinement — all this should be enough to convince us that something profoundly shocking must have occurred.

Little wonder therefore that the tragic personality of the great

Rabbi of Kotzk attracted so many writers and researchers. All of them faced the same insurmountable difficulty of tracing genetically and presenting coherently a story for which there is insufficient source material. So many of the chasidic writers took the road of least resistance and recorded an uncritical account as transmitted by chasidic tradition.

Only one monograph, which partially fulfills our desire for a discriminating evaluation of the Rabbi of Kotzk's life story, has come to attention. We refer to I. Arigur's Hebrew volume entitled *Kotzk* (Tel Aviv, 1935). In addition, there are also a few worthwhile articles scattered through a number of Hebrew periodicals.

An invaluable service has been performed by a group that termed itself "an assemblage of young men whose aim is to collect, edit, and publish the teachings, utterances, discourses, life stories, and accomplishments of the rabbis, the great men of chasiduth." In the *Amud Ha'Emet* that they published (Tel Aviv, no year of publication given), they collected, from twenty-odd sources, all the utterances and anecdotes attributed to Rabbi Menachem Mendel of Kotzk. The reader who is not satisfied with second-hand accounts and desires to get acquainted with the original materials has thus been given an opportunity to satisfy his curiosity. Nevertheless, this collection is insufficient for the researcher, because the pious collectors have "edited" and abbreviated certain sayings, and thus deprived them of their original color. A reading of some of these quotations in their divergent settings provides a glimpse into the mood and frame of mind of their originator.

The chasidic rabbis of earlier times rarely expressed their thoughts directly, and never recorded their ideas in a systematic, coherent manner. Their opinions and views were usually hidden in Torah utterances and in commentaries on Scriptural or Talmudic phrases. Rabbi Menachem Mendel of Kotzk was no exception to this rule, although here and there he spoke his mind freely, without the usual embellishments. The reader is struck by the vigor of his ideas, and the expressiveness of his epigrams and remarks. Behind the traditional garb of a chasidic "tzaddik" was a man of keen insight, penetrating mind, and revolutionary ideas.

A careful and dispassionate analysis of the ideas of the Rabbi of Kotzk, as has been attempted by the author of this study, will prove that Rabbi Menachem Mendel was misunderstood by all of his contemporaries — followers and antagonists alike. With his keen mental perception, he anticipated the ideas that became current a generation later among the research scholars engaged in the scientific study of Jewish intellectual history. It was the tragedy of the lonely man of Kotzk that he was venerated but little understood by his followers, and completely misjudged by his opponents.

Only today, a century after the passing of the "tragic figure of chasidic agony," as Martin Buber characterizes him, is it possible to reconsider and reevaluate the teachings of this misinterpreted man and place them in proper historic perspective. And this is what the author of this book has done. Students of chasidic history, and readers who will for the first time come in touch with the personality of the great man of Kotzk, will find in this book a refreshing and penetrating account of the life of one of the greatest teachers that pre-modern Jewry had produced.

Chapter 1

Polish Jewry (1745-1815)

The sources of chasiduth are deeply rooted in the subsoil of Jewish history. All the previous centuries of Jewish life and thought serve as a background for the proper understanding of the chasidic ideology and message. However, the immediate causes that stimulated the chasidic movement's emergence lie in the peculiar political, social, and economic conditions created by the steadily ongoing process of disintegration of the Polish Kingdom.

With the anarchy which engulfed the Kingdom of Poland after the Cossack uprising, inspired by Bogdan Chmielnicki (1648), and the ensuing wars with Russia and Sweden began a chain of developments which culminated in the complete dismemberment of Poland and its gradual partition among its three neighbors, Russia, Prussia, and Austria (1772-1815). These political defeats were only the external manifestation of the inner decay of that country and the impropriety of its social order. The ruling aristocracy, concerned only with the preservation of its privileges, showed little interest in the needs of the state and the welfare of its population. The kings, deprived of their legislative and executive authority, were no longer in a position to exercise the moderating influence that assured the Jews some measure of protection and justice. The kings of the Saxon dynasty (1697-1763) ratified the old Jewish privileges, but in the prevailing state of anarchy all royal enactments remained mere scraps of paper. Rights granted in writing meant very little in a country that had no government ready to enforce those rights. The royal officials, who were duty-bound to execute the country's laws, were frequently their most flagrant violators. They showed no respect for their own laws and boasted of the fact that "Poland stands by lawlessness."

The government showed concern for its Jewish subjects only when it came to the collection of the Jewish head-tax. The prolonged period of unrest pauperized the Jews, wiping out about one-third of the Jewish population. These facts notwithstanding, the Diet of 1764 quadrupled the amount of taxes levied on them.[1] The partitions of Poland and the Napoleonic wars brought a change for the worse. Each one of the three partitioning governments pursued its own policy towards the Jews. Albeit, one thing all of them had in common: they regarded the Jews primarily as a source of potential income.

The payment of taxes to the central government was only a fraction of what the Jews had to spend in order to keep alive. It was a common practice among the provincial representatives of government, whenever in need of money, to turn to their local Jewish communities. If the Jews refused to pay the sum imposed on them, their community leaders were put in jail and held there until the levy was paid in full. The meetings of the provincial diets and the sessions of the court tribunals were occasions for attacking Jews, invading their synagogues and houses, and engaging in all kinds of "amusements" that brought them suffering.

One Polish aristocrat used to order Jewish women to climb an apple tree and call like cuckoos. He would then practice target shooting and fire at them with a small rifle. Then, laughing merrily, he would throw gold coins on the wounded victims.[2] The Polish aristocratic families often engaged in family squabbles and petty warfare, and intentionally or unintentionally, the Jews were the main sufferers. One noble, desiring to avenge the murder of his Jewish *arendar,* ordered the capture of Jews inhabiting the neighboring village, loaded them on a wagon, and threw them down like bags of potatoes at the gates of the palace of his adversary. It was the common practice of Polish nobles to keep imprisoned in their pigpens the Jewish *arendars* who were unable to pay their rent. The unfortunates were set free only when the Jews from the neighboring towns collected among themselves the amount claimed by the aristocrat. At times, the young children of the incarcerated Jew were taken to the noble's court and forced to accept the Catholic faith.

The prevailing anarchy and breakdown of the law enforcement apparatus encouraged looting and highway robbery. The records of the Lublin Jewish community state that a special functionary was assigned to look after Jews murdered on the country roads and provide them with a Jewish burial.[3]

At one time the Polish nobility even made an attempt to convert into serfs all the Jews who lived on their estates. At the Diet of 1740 a bill was introduced to recognize, as "hereditary subjects" of the estate owners, all the Jews who dwelled on their premises. This law was not enacted, solely because the king refused to forgo the income from Jewish taxation — which would then flow, instead, into the pockets of the landowners. Nevertheless, for all practical purposes the small town and village Jews remained the undisputed property of the nobles; the latter were free to do with their Jews whatever they pleased. This situation changed at only about the middle of the nineteenth century, when the partitioning governments successfully introduced law and order in their Polish provinces.

The Jews of the crown cities were not much better off. Many cities protected themselves against the settlement of Jews in their midst by the clinging to their medieval *privilegium de non tolerandis Judaeis*. All over the country the Jews were engaged in endless litigation with the Christian merchants and craft guilds, who, in many cases, successfully expelled the Jews from the central business areas and then restrained their freedom of trade. The Diet of 1768 made the right of the Jews to engage in commerce subject to the approval of the local city governments — and these consisted of Christian merchants who were sure to uphold their rights against the Jews.[4] Whenever the Christian merchants felt that their Jewish competitors were getting ahead of them, they called the mob into action. The ensuing plunder and destruction of Jewish property gave them, for a time, the aspired economic advantage they were unable to achieve by legal means.

All these actions reduced sharply the field of Jewish economic activity. There were only a few rich Jews, and these were mostly engaged in export trade. According to an official investigation conducted in 1788, the mass of the Jews of Poland consisted of petty traders, storekeepers, shoemakers, tailors, furriers, carpenters, and stonecutters, who traded with and worked for the surrounding farm population. Though the Jews formed only one-eighth of the inhabitants of Poland, they furnished 50% of the whole number of artisans, and 75% of them engaged in export trade.

But all these occupations were obviously insufficient for their maintenance. One-twelfth of the Jewish population was made up of "idlers" without a definite occupation, while one-sixtieth

16

consisted of beggars.⁵ The living expenses of the Jewish businessman were half as large as those of the Christian merchant of the corresponding social class; only this life of poverty enabled the Jew to sell his goods cheaper and stay in business in spite of all the odds against him.

The constant clashes with the Christian middle class and the legal restrictions imposed upon the Jewish trade forced many enterprising Jews out of the cities and into the manors of the landowners. Here they hoped to find economic opportunity and legal protection against discriminative official practices. As a rule, the Polish nobles, engaged in politics and petty warfare, gave little personal attention to the administration of their estates. Many Jews made fortunes in leasing from the noble landowners the various items of agricultural wealth, such as dairies and pasture lands, timber, grain fields, and most important of all, the "propination" — the right of distilling and selling liquor.

These pursuits often resulted in clashes between the "favored" Jews and other, less fortunate Jews, who did not know how to ingratiate themselves with the nobles and win from them economic advantages. In many instances the unscrupulous Jew, bound neither by the regulations nor ethics of Jewish law, cooperated with the nobility against the interests of many of his fellow Jews. The nobleman's patronage gave this Jew a position of leadership within the Jewish community, and this was resented bitterly by the poor and wronged. This situation undermined the authority of the official community leadership, and was one of the factors that fed the fires of the chasidic "revolt."

In their campaign for the restriction of the Jews' economic position, the Polish merchant and craftsman found an enthusiastic ally in the Catholic clergy. The seed sown by the Jesuit

17

schoolmasters, who controlled the Polish school system, yielded a rich harvest. Religious intolerance, hypocrisy, and superstition had taken deep root in the Polish people. Religious persecution directed against the Jews, "who stubbornly cling to irreligion," was among the most popular pursuits that caught the imagination of the Poles during the period of their country's political disintegration. The enactments of the synods of Catholic clergy were reminiscent of the Middle Ages. The Synod of 1733 held in Plotzk repeated the well-known Church maxim: the only reason for tolerating the Jews in a Christian country is that they might serve as a "reminder of the tortures of Christ and, by their enslaved and miserable position, as an example of the just chastisement inflicted by God upon the infidels."[6]

Inevitably, this resurrection of the spirit of the Middle Ages brought back to life all the medieval accusations against the Jews. The last century of Poland's existence was marked by the frequency of religious trials, the Jews being charged with ritual murder and the desecration of Church sacraments. In some cases these charges were the indigenous product of the superstition and ignorance of the masses. However, in many instances the clergy and the Christian merchants had a direct hand in setting up the crime in order to be rid of their Jewish competitors. Libels of this kind usually led to street riots, destruction and plunder of Jewish property, burning of synagogues, and the imprisonment and execution of the Jewish community's leading men. The Jews were always the losers in these trials, because the Polish tribunals kept the witnesses for years, applying to them all the tortures available in the apparatus of the Inquisition, until the witnesses finally broke down and admitted whatever they were forced to admit. The Sandomir Trial (1698-1710) ended with the execution of the accused, the expulsion of the Jews from the city, and the conversion of the synagogue into a Catholic chapel. In order to keep posterity informed about the crime of the Jews, the Catholic clergy placed a revolting picture representing the scene of the ritual murder in the local church.

In a particularly bad situation were the Jews of the southeastern Polish provinces of Volhynia, Podolia, and the Ukraine. Nothing had radically changed here since the times of the Chmielnicki massacres (1648-49). The Jew always found himself in the midst of the class, religious, and national struggle of the Poles and Ukrainians. He was despised and hated by both sides and dealt with mercilessly whenever the two came to an armed clash. The inner anarchy and disorganization of Poland encouraged the Cossacks from the Russian part of the Ukraine to raid the bordering countryside, loot the estates of the Polish aristocrats, and plunder and kill the Jews of the towns. These *haidamack* incursions assumed the character of regular warfare during the interregna and on the occasions of strained Polish-Russian relationships. Particularly bloody was the *haidamack* movement of 1768, which ended in the slaughter of the entire Jewish community of Uman.

The Jews of Poland, despite the general disintegration of the country, were still able to hold their own as an organized social unit, due mainly to the vast scheme of communal self-government which had become an integral part of Polish Jewish life during the preceding period. The Polish government preferred to deal with the total national Jewish community rather than with the manifold local communities or individual Jews. This attitude of the government strengthened the national, provincial, and local community councils, and invested them with vast administrative and judicial powers. Almost all areas of economic activity became subject to community regulations, and the adjudication of all litigation arising between individual Jews, or between a Jew and the community, was vested in the hands of the rabbinate. Among the most important duties of the *kahal* (community council) were the supervision and maintenance of Jewish schools, on the elementary and higher levels, and the exercise of control over Jewish spiritual life. This tutelage of the *kahal* consequently strengthened the social cohesion of the Jews, while at the same time curbing their personal liberty and freedom of movement.

The entire *kahal* organization received a severe blow at the hands of the Polish government in 1764, eight years before the first partition of Poland. The government had decided to change fundamentally the whole system of taxation. Instead of levying a fixed amount of head-tax on the entire Polish-Jewish population and leaving its distribution to the national conference of the communities, the government imposed a uniform tax of two gulden on every Jewish soul and made the local communities responsible for its collection. This government action resulted in the dissolution of the centralized Jewish self-government and left each local community virtually on its own. The ensuing partitions of Poland and the Napoleonic wars weakened still further the community organizations, and gave dissenting elements within the communities a relative freedom to act on their own, without paying much heed to established tradition and rabbinic opinion.

The unsettled condition on the southeastern Polish frontier and the recurrent invasions of Cossacks and Tartars brought a never-ending stream of refugees to the more secure communities farther removed from the border. This influx of newcomers aggravated the difficult enough economic situation of the old, settled population. The entire country lay in a state of chaos and disorganization. Everyone struggled to make ends meet; the Jewish communities were engaged in a defensive battle with the Christian merchants and craft guilds for every economic position held by the Jews.

In this time of scarcity, it was nearly impossible to find economic opportunities for the newcomers. The Jewish community issued laws which protected the economic rights of the old settlers against the unfair competition of the new arrivals. Under these circumstances, the refugees were pushed down to the ranks of an urban proletariat, with no steady occupation or social position. We know that Israel Ba'al Shem Tov, the founder of the chasidic movement, came from such a family.[7]

The breakup of Polish society and the aristocracy's evident complete disregard for the other classes adversely affected the Jewish social scene. The class differences within the Jewish communities continued to increase and assume aggravating dimensions. The merchants and storekeepers began to look down on the craftsmen and laborers, and refused to associate with them. Jews who made a living by manual labor were considered socially and culturally inferior — a situation unheard of in the previous period.

The constant invasions, inner warfare, and mob riots ruined many of the old, wealthy families in which affluence accompanied Torah learning and social responsibility. A class of *nouveau riche* arose, which lacked the cultural refinement and social consciousness of the people it replaced. The Polish noblemen, whom they served as business agents, helped them take over the *kahal* leadership; this newly won distinction soon became an opportunity for economic advantage. The *kahal*

21

administration joined hands with the Polish officials in ruthlessly exploiting the helpless population. The entire institution of Jewish self-government became a mockery.

The sermonic literature (*musar*) of the period abounds with exhortations against the leaders "who split with the noblemen the money they have taken away from the Jews."[8] A Jew who applies to them for assistance can never receive it, because "they are constantly preoccupied with their businesses; they have dealings with aristocratic men and women and are busy with the pursuit of their pleasures." With the assistance of their highly placed patrons they force themselves as leaders upon the communities and the Jews must accept them, "because the Jews are nowadays a persecuted and impoverished nation."

The *kahal's* main function was the collection of government taxes. Now the ordinary people began to suspect that their elders collected from them more than required by law. "Our leaders, heads, and elders allow themselves to eat from the treasury of the community . . . they impose upon the plain people taxes and levies more than required, and they deal harshly with Israel. They have acquired the 'nobleman's manners' of favoring the rich and showing contempt for the poor."

The rabbinate could not escape the pervading atmosphere of corruption and decay. Many noblemen, on whose land Jewish communities were established, made it a practice to approve their community's choice of rabbi. Soon they became the dispensers of rabbinic offices, and the office of rabbi went to the candidate that presented them with the highest amount of money. The Jews lost all respect for these rabbis, and accused them of scheming with the landowner and *kahal* elders against the community interests.

In many instances the *kahal* leader succeeded in winning the rabbinic appointment for his son or son-in-law, and the community lost all trust in the impartiality of its rabbi's judicial decisions. The *musar* literature complains bitterly against "the rabbis who buy from the landowners their office and then they oppress their people, rob the skin and flesh from their bones." Not too many rabbis succeeded in these harsh times at maintaining their integrity and their people's confidence.

The available records clearly indicate the undercurrent of revolt against the supremacy of the community leaders and rabbis among the oppressed Jewish masses. The farther away from the great urban Jewish centers, the more befogged were the conditions, widespread the corruption, and vociferous the outcry against the official leadership.

The crisis reached its summit in the southeastern Polish provinces, where the rebellion against official Judaism openly emerged in the form of the Frankist challenge (1757). Many of these Jews, having lived for generations in a Greek Orthodox environment, were influenced by its outspoken contempt for learning and by its glorification of humble, blissful ignorance.

All these political, economic, and social factors were augmented by the spiritual crisis which enveloped eighteenth-century Jewry as a result of the failure of the Shabbatai Zevi messianic venture and the lack of vitality of rabbinic theology, with which the next chapter will deal. Keeping in mind all these circumstances which affected the unique situation of Polish Jewry in the era of the disintegration of the Polish Kingdom, we will be able to better understand the origin, the message, and the rapid spread of the chasidic movement.

Chapter 1 — Notes

For more intensive study of the material contained in this and in the following chapter, the reader is referred to Simon Dubnow's trailblazing work *Toldot HaChasidut* (The History of Chasiduth). Background material can also be found in an earlier work of the author that has been translated into English: *History of the Jews in Russia and Poland.* Jacob Minkin's *The Romance of Hasidism* is informative, though at times enthusiastic and subjective in tone and evaluation.

1. Dubnow, *Toldot HaChasidut,* p. 9
2. Dubnow, *History of the Jews in Russia and Poland,* vol. 1, p. 169
3. Horodetzky, S. H. A., *HaChasidut VeHaChasidim,* Introduction, p. 49
4. Dubnow, *History,* p. 182
5. Dubnow, *History,* p. 263
6. Dubnow, *Toldot HaChasidut,* pp. 13-14
7. Benzion Dinaburg, *Reshita shel HaChasidut Ve'Yesodoteha HaSozialiim Ve'HaMeshichiim,* in *Zion,* vol. 9 (1935), p. 89
8. Dinaburg, *l. c.,* vol. 8, pp. 125-134

Chapter 2

The Rise of the Chasidic Movement

Professor Abraham J. Heschel, in his noteworthy appreciation of the historic destiny of East European Jewish history, written under the terrible impact of the Nazi holocaust, recorded the following momentous lines:

> Classical books were not written in Eastern Europe. The Talmud, the *Mishneh Torah*, the *Book of Splendor*, the *Guide of the Perplexed*, and the *Tree of Life* were produced in other countries. East European Jewry lacked the ambition to create consummate, definitive, perfect expressions. Their books were so rooted in a self-contained world that they are less accessible to moderns than the books of the Sephardic authors. They are not literature; they read like notes of discussions with pupils. They did not write books that stand like separate buildings with foundations of their own; all their works lean upon older books, are commentaries on classical works of ancient time, modestly hug the monumental walls of old citadels of learning.
>
> In their lives everything was fixed according to a certain pattern, nothing was casual, nothing was left to chance. But they also had sufficient vitality constantly to modify the accepted pattern. New customs were continually added to, and the old customs enriched with fresh nuances. The form and ceremonies were passed on from generation to generation, but the meaning which was attached to them did not remain the same. A perennial source gave renewed life to tradition.[1]

Chasiduth was an aspect of this perennial source of rejuvenation of Jewish life. It emerged in the 18th century, in Poland, as a reaction to the sterility and stagnation that cloaked a large segment of the Jewish population. While the larger communities in Poland proper recovered, at least spiritually and intellectually, from the ceaseless wars and ensuing anarchy, the Jews who inhabited the border provinces of Podolia, Volhynia, and the Ukraine remained prostrated, and wounds inflicted upon them were never healed.

Many of these Jews lived in villages and noblemen's estates, far away from an organized Jewish community. Constantly in an environment of Greek Orthodox peasants, they were gradually influenced by the latter's habits and beliefs. As a result, the religious life of these small Jewish outposts became encrusted with all kinds of bizarre customs and superstitious beliefs. Thus a rift ensued between the learned city Jew and the ignorant village Jew, to whom all sources of a formal book education were inaccessible.

When on the High Holidays the villager came to the city to join in the community services, he quite often sensed that he was unwelcome, and felt out of place. The rabbi's sermon was not intended for the education and spiritual uplift of the masses, but directed, instead, to the learned part of the audience, which was able to appreciate his erudition and clever juggling of quotations. The village Jew felt uncomfortable in this erudite and formal Jewish community and synagogue life, in which only the rich and the learned had a part. Conscious of the scorn and non-acceptance that the leading spokesmen of the Jewish community harbored towards them, the uneducated strayed away from the beaten path of accepted Jewish behavior. The subconscious antagonism between the two classes of Jews deepened and widened daily.

Nevertheless, the religious feelings and piety remained very strong in the hearts of the masses. Their starved religious emotions found satisfaction in mysticism and superstition. Toviah Ha-

Cohen, a physician of the latter half of the seventeenth century, described the people's mentality in these words: "There is no country in the world where people occupy themselves more with evil spirits, amulets, exorcism, holy names, and dreams as they do in Poland."[2] On account of their proximity to Turkey, the southern Polish provinces were exposed more than the others to the influences of the Lurian Kabbala and the messianic movement of Shabbatai Zevi. The former preached asceticism and the destruction of carnal pleasures; the latter usually brought about a laxity of observance and moral degeneration.

The then-popular *musar* literature provides us with an excellent portrayal of the mass mind. People were preoccupied with the Last Judgment and the World to Come. The slightest infringement upon an accepted custom was to be punished by years and years of exposure to the torments of Hell. Hosts of demons were thirsting for the blood of sinners whose souls had been waiting for redemption. To free themselves of these oppressing fears the people sought the help of the *Ba'al Shem* (The Master of the Name), who was believed able to perform miracles, heal the sick, and exorcise demons by his skill in combining letters that spelled out the Ineffable Name. The Ba'al Shem represented a kind of a mixture of medicine man and Kabbalist, who composed amulets, prescribed medicine, and drove out evil spirits.

Such was the world in which chasiduth arose. In this environment there grew up a man, Israel Ba'al Shem Tov (1700-1760, Besht in abbreviation), who breathed a new spirit into the beliefs and traditions current in his days. He brought forth a new religious movement that reanimated and revolutionized the religious and social outlook of vast segments of East European Jewry.

The life of the founder of the chasidic movement is shrouded in mystery and encircled with a halo of legend. These legendary stories tell us little about his accomplishments in Talmudic studies. As a child he disliked the gloomy atmosphere of the *cheder* (religious school) and escaped into the woods, where he lingered for long hours, absorbed in deep thought. His superiors lost patience with him and allowed him to do as he pleased. When he grew up, he was an apprenticed assistant to a schoolmaster. He won the hearts of the little children by chanting hymns with them out of doors, and telling them wonderful stories under the green trees of the forest. Israel Ba'al Shem attained his spiritual maturity not in the house of study, but in the woods and wild ravines of the Carpathian Mountains. He had no celebrated rabbi as his master, and never claimed distinction in Talmudic learning. According to legend, he spent his nights devouring Kabbala books and penetrating their hidden mysteries. He was his own teacher. If not self-taught, it was from angelic lips, or even from the Divine voice itself, that he gleaned the higher knowledge.

The time for the revelation of his identity finally arrived in 1736. He became a *Ba'al Shem,* a healer of the sick and a miracle-worker. He traveled around the towns and villages, mingling with the peasants, innkeepers, brewers, and petty traders, participating in their sorrows and joys. He captivated their hearts with sympathetic understanding of their problems, and with his generosity, piety, and art of storytelling. He liked good horses, and frequently went around the fairs examining rare specimens with the air of an experienced horse dealer.

About the year 1745, the Besht entered upon the final stage of his career. He ceased to travel as a *Ba'al Shem,* and moved to Medzhibozh, in Podolia. Here he became the center of a new

28

movement, whose followers were called by the old name of chasidim. The number of his admirers began to increase, and people came to him from near and far not only to be cured or helped, but to listen to his teachings.

Neither Israel Ba'al Shem Tov nor his early disciples made a conscious attempt to present the principles of chasiduth in a systematic way. All we have are collections of stories, aphorisms, remarks, and interpretations of Biblical and post-Biblical passages, and from these we must draw our own generalizations.

The keynote to all the teachings of the Besht is the omnipresence of God. The idea of the constant living presence of God in all existence permeates his every word and deed. The phrase "I place God before me always" (Psalms 16:8) was to him literal truth. His strongest desire was union with Him. It was the prime passion and motif of his life, and expressed itself in concentrated thought, devotion, study, and prayer.

There is nothing that is void of God. The Holy One sent his *Shechinah* (Divine Glory) upon the earth; its sparks are in all things, material and immaterial. God is in the simple and ignorant heart of the peasant, as He is in the wisdom and learning of the scholar. The word of God perpetually speaks, acts, and generates throughout heaven and earth, in endless gradations and variations. The vivifying power of God is never withdrawn from the world which it animates. Creation is continuous, as is also revelation. This revelation is only to be grasped by faith. Faith, therefore, is more valuable than learning.

Since God is in everything, it follows that there is good — actual or potential — in all things. Sin and evil are not absolute conditions, but relative, and may be turned into goodness and virtue. God is regained in a moment of repentance, and he who leads the sinner to repentance causes a Divine joy. It is as though a king's son who had been in captivity has been brought back to his father.

From this attitude flows the Ba'al Shem's optimism. Whereas the Lurian Kabbala taught penance and mortification of the flesh, chasiduth insisted that man should approach his Creator with happiness and joy. When he heard that one of his disciples was following ascetic practices, the Ba'al Shem wrote to him: "By the counsel of God, I order you to abandon such dangerous practices, which are but the outcome of a discorded mind. It is written, 'Hide not yourself from your own flesh' (Isaiah 58:7). Fast, then, no more than is prescribed; follow my command and God will be with you."[3]

From here we come to a consideration of the Besht's view of prayer. He is reputed to have said that all the greatness he had achieved was due not to study but to prayer.[4] Prayer is that sense of unity with God which elevates man to higher spheres and divests him of his corporeality. Prayer must be devout, enthusiastic, and rapturous. It is an act of Divine mercy that man can survive the experience of such exalted prayer. In prayer we should ask not for favors and petitions, but merely to be admitted into His presence. Since prayer is inward, its external forms do not matter. Time and place are not important.

The reader should be cautioned here against ascribing to the Besht any modern rationalistic notions on the subject of prayer. He had no doubt about the power of prayer to produce an answer from God. He felt, however, that any reference to earthly requirements was destructive to the communion of man with God. The wise man does not trouble the King with innumerable petitions about trifles. His desire is merely to gain admission into the King's presence and to speak to Him without a go-between.[5]

The road to union with God through prayer is open not only to the learned but also to the ignorant, who do not comprehend the meaning of the Hebrew words their lips utter in devotion. The founders of chasiduth placed emphasis on three attributes of prayer and piety: *kavanah, d'vekuth,* and *hithlahavuth.* By *kavanah*, they meant the intensity of feeling and complete absorption in the pious mood that makes one oblivious to physical surroundings. Although *kavanah* comes through the grace of God, it can be stimulated by letting the meaning of the prayer flow into one's soul before pronouncing any words.

D'vekuth is that cleaving unto God in which separation from Him in any way is inconceivable. Prayer is the promise of which *d'vekuth* is the fulfillment. By the means of *d'vekuth*, prayer ceases to be routine and becomes a refreshing and ennobling experience. Swaying of the body was usually employed to help bring about the state of *d'vekuth.*

Hithlahavuth is the kindling and purifying fire which saves religion from stagnating into cold formality. Prayer without *hithlahavuth* is like the wood upon the altar before it is touched by the heavenly fire. *Hithlahavuth* melts away the dualism of the corporeal and incorporeal. It is that ecstasy which spans a bridge between heaven and earth, and man becomes one with the Living Soul of Eternity.

Israel Ba'al Shem Tov preached three kinds of love: love of God, love of Israel, and love of Torah. By love of Israel he meant not the abstract, overall love of the people as a whole, but a love for each individual Jew, no matter how humble and simple he might be. He mingled with all sorts of men, especially the social outcasts and the poor. It was told that before he went to sleep he distributed among the poor and needy all the money that had come to him during the day.

By love of Torah the Besht meant the fulfillment of the oral and written law which make for the sanctity of life. He put little stress upon the continual and uninterrupted study of Talmud. He accepted, of course, the belief that the Torah was a revelation of God. But as the world itself is equally a Divine revelation, the Torah is just part of a larger whole. To understand it properly, one needs to penetrate to the infinite light which is revealed in it. Study of the Torah is no end in itself, but a means of inspiration. The object of the whole Torah is that man should become similar to the Torah. He should love God and be united with Him. Every action of man should be a pure manifestation of God. The important thing is not how many separate commandments a man obeys, but how and in what spirit they are obeyed.

This ideal, that man should become like the Torah, leads us to the concept of the *tzaddik,* the man who has become the clear manifestation of God on earth. "The tzaddik is the messenger of the Shechinah."[6] He is the connecting bond between God and His creatures. He is the source of blessing and the fountain of grace. "The will of the tzaddik agrees with the will of God," said his disciple, the Maggid of Meseritz.

Thus went the teachings of Israel Ba'al Shem Tov. Gershom G. Scholem states that this burst of mystical energy, which we call chasiduth, was devoid of new religious ideas and added nothing to the accumulated theories of mystical knowledge. The chasidim themselves were aware of this fact. Even the rise and doctrine of tzaddikim appeared to them as being, despite apparent novelty, well in the Kabbalistic tradition.

Therefore, the new element introduced by chasiduth must not

be sought on the theoretical and literary plane, but rather in the experience of an inner revival. Chasiduth successfully energized and revitalized spiritual ideas that were more or less well known, and converted them into a stimulus for a mass movement. It was not the system of ideas that gave its specific color to the movement. In fact, the great majority of its followers was completely ignorant of any specific set of ideas, but experienced the glow of faith and vitality that chasiduth released. It thus became a motivating force in the everyday life of its adherents.[7]

With the exception of the Chabad system, to which we shall refer later, chasiduth seems to have produced no truly original Kabbalistic thought whatever. The focal point of the mystical investigation was moved from the realm of theosophy to that of the personal life. Chasiduth is practical mysticism at its peak. Almost all the Kabbalistic ideas are now placed in relation to values peculiar to the individual life, and those which are not remain empty and ineffective. Thus, chasiduth represents "Kabbalism turned Ethos."

Chasiduth is "a mysticism which hallows community and everyday life."[8]

Chapter 2 — Notes

1. Quoted after Abraham J. Heschel, *The Inner World of the Polish Jew,* p. 8.
2. Dubnow, *History of the Jews in Russia and Poland,* vol. 1, p. 203
3. Quoted from Minkin, *The Romance of Hasidism,* p. 88
4. Dubnow, *Toldot HaChasidut,* p. 55
5. Schechter, Solomon, "The Chasidim," pp. 1-45, in *Studies in Judaism,* v. 1, p. 24
6. Waxman, Meyer, *A History of Jewish Literature,* vol. 2, p. 38
7. Scholem, Gershom G., *Major Trends in Jewish Mysticism,* pp. 338-342
8. Buber, Martin, *Hasidism and Modern Man,* p. 10

Chapter 3

The Ukrainian, White-Russian, and Polish Schools of Chasiduth

Israel Ba'al Shem Tov was determined to expand the chasidic movement and win over the entire Jewish people. He staunchly believed that by doing so he would hasten the coming of Messiah. In a letter addressed to his brother-in-law, Gershon Kitover, he mentioned that on Rosh Hashana his soul ascended "the upper worlds" and entered the chamber of Messiah. He asked the Messiah: "When will you come?" and received the following answer: "By this shall you know, when your teachings will become known and be revealed to the world, and your wings will spread all over, and all [will accept] that which I have taught you . . . then will impurity perish and there will be a time of willingness and salvation."[1] This vision fired the missionary zeal of the chasidim, and they set out to convert all of East European Jewry to their way of life.

During the founder's life, chasiduth had drawn adherents mainly from the intellectually lower classes of society. However, his successor, Rabbi Dov Baer, the Maggid (preacher) of Meseritz, attracted to himself many of the most learned young men of his generation. The expansion of chasiduth was chiefly due to these new and ardent converts. Rabbi Dov Baer was a

34

Talmudist who knew the world and knew how to win people over. If chasiduth was to live and expand, it had to win the support of the learned. This was probably the thinking of the Besht during the last years of his life; this was why he befriended the Maggid and passed on to him the mantle of leadership.

The expansion of chasiduth during the following half-century, and its penetration into almost all East European communities, were due mainly to Rabbi Dov Baer's organizational talents. Judiciously, he dedicated the twelve years of his stewardship (1760-1772) to training the movement's future leaders. Large crowds gathered daily at his door but he deliberately avoided them. Only on the Sabbath did he take time to show himself to the masses. According to the testimony of his contemporaries, each of his appearances left a profound impression, and his sermons were well-received and remembered. These public functions, from which no chasidic leader could in good grace excuse himself, were kept to the bare minimum. During the weekdays, all of his waking hours were devoted to inculcating his chosen group of scholars with the ideas of chasiduth. Some of these men were sent to the nearby communities as itinerant preachers. "They wandered from town to town, and everywhere they sought out men of heart and flesh and turned them to God and urged them to go to Meseritz."[2]

Among this group of disciples was a number of men of discriminating minds and independent judgment, and it is quite astounding to read about the lasting effect Rabbi Dov Baer left upon them. One of these, the famous Rabbi Levi Yitzchak of Berditchev, recalled years later how he was overawed by the very presence of the Great Maggid and the tense religious atmosphere that prevailed in his court. He wrote down in a diary every word that fell from his master's lips. He found the deepest wisdom in his master's every utterance, and mysterious significance in the very movements of his body. Once, on Rosh Hashana, Levi Yitzchak even claimed to have seen a halo around the Maggid's head.[3]

Rabbi Shneur Zalman, the founder of the Chabad system, was all aglow when he recalled his Meseritz experiences. He recalled that when Rabbi Dov Baer expounded his chasidic teachings he was completely divested of his corporeality and the Divine Spirit spoke through him. Once he noticed that somebody descended from above and engaged the Maggid in a prolonged conversation. This was none other than Rabbi Isaac Luria, the founder of the Practical Kabbala system.

Rabbi Dov Baer did not add anything of his own to chasidic theory. He merely repeated the teachings of his master. Only in one aspect did he make a contribution: he expanded vastly the position of the tzaddik. Basing his claim upon the verse: "The tzaddik (righteous man) is the foundation of the world" (Proverbs 10:25), he ascribed to him dominion over the spiritual and material world. The tzaddik is not only symbolic of the ideal life, but is also invested with the power of extracting the will and favor of God. As the seed draws its sustenance from the earth, so does the tzaddik derive his spiritual authority from the Heavenly Throne. The tzaddik is the pillar between heaven and earth, through which all the profusion from the upper world descends to this world. By his intercession with God, he can secure forgiveness for sins. The Divine sparks inherent in matter reveal to him their secrets, and by his touch profane things become sanctified. He has the power to confer or withhold material blessings. The chasid should, therefore, cling to his tzaddik as a child cleaves to its mother.[4]

The theory of "tzaddikism" was still further enlarged by one of the Maggid's disciples, Rabbi Elimelech of Lizensk (deceased 1786). Rabbi Elimelech claimed that the tzaddik is a peer to the angels, and through the touch of his hands the bitter becomes sweet. The tzaddik knows how to combine the letters and words of the prayers in such a way as to reflect through them God's will. Through the powers of his prayer he can, therefore, cure the sick and also prolong a man's life, even if it were God's will that he should die. To the tzaddik was granted the secret knowledge of investing worldly occurrences with the holiness of the Ineffable Name, which constitutes their inner essence. Thus, when a chasid asks the tzaddik for a cure or for a livelihood, his request will be fulfilled because the tzaddik has caused the name of God to penetrate into these things. The word of the tzaddik is obeyed by God; the tzaddik decrees and God puts the decree into effect. In every generation God obeys the tzaddik, as the servant listens to his master. The tzaddikim are the holy ones to whom God commanded the children of Israel to bring their offerings. It is through the strength of these gifts that the tzaddik is enabled to procure an assurance and abundance of blessings for his followers.[5]

The doctrine of the tzaddik as the intermediary between God and man soon became the distinguishing feature of chasiduth. As understood by East European Jews, the designation "chasid" did not connote that its bearer held certain distinct opinions in matters of belief, but that he was a devotee of a certain tzaddik. Chasiduth thus degenerated into "tzaddikism" and its subsequent history was tied up with the proliferation of the multifarious dynasties of tzaddikim. When the intense outburst of deep religiosity characterizing the birth of chasiduth was converted into a social movement, it was inevitable that the mystic/saint, its leader, came to personify the lofty mystical ideas of piety, love, devotion, trust, and even greatness and domination. As the head of a group, the tzaddik̇ had to employ all these mystical attributes for the service and welfare of the largest numbers. The essential difference between the earlier Kabbala and the later chasiduth lay in the fact that the Kabbalists guarded their mystery and admitted to it only a few chosen spirits; chasiduth, on the other hand, had always in mind the masses, and attempted to affect their thinking and everyday behavior.

As leaders of a mass movement, the chasidic greats had of necessity to yield to the wishes of the masses. And these multitudes of uneducated, disenfranchised, oppressed, and very often hunted Jews yearned for leaders who possessed the power of carrying their prayers to the Heavenly Throne and wrangling from God the necessities of everyday life. Thus, in arrogating to themselves all these mysterious prerogatives, the tzaddikim fulfilled the expressed and unexpressed yearnings of their constituencies, who clamored for practical messiahs to ease the burdens of exile. If we accept Martin Buber's definition that chasiduth was "Kabbalism turned Ethos," it soon turned out to be, after the passing of its "heroic period," "Kabbalism turned Tzaddikism."

This development does not necessarily imply that all tzaddikim were merely hungry miracle-performers who imposed upon their people and dulled their ethical and intellectual sensitivities. There were among them many outstanding personalities who approached the Besht's ideal of a mystic/saint. These tzaddikim left a lasting impression on the movement and became living incarnations of the chasidic ideal. The intensity of creative religious feelings, when combined with the ethical and intellectual keenness of Talmudic learning, created a great number of truly religious personalities. They inspired all who came in contact with them to rise to higher levels of religious feeling and living. The heroic period produced a flowering of such personalities. However, as time went on, the sources of inspiration dried up and frequently the commonplace supplanted the authentic mystical experience. Rabbi Menachem Mendel of Kotzk, to whom this study is devoted, might well have been the last of the great chasidic mystics.

Here we have a classic controversy on determining what shapes human history: Are the changes in the course of human affairs due mainly to the influences of the leader, who gives rise to a new set of accepted ideas, or to the impact of the peculiar conditions of the age and environment that produce their spokesmen? This time-honored dilemma could partially be answered in the light of the rise and development of the chasidic movement.

The outstanding feature of chasiduth is the attraction of the inspired leader's personality to the mass of believers. The leaders draw their exaltation and eminence not from their immediate surroundings, but from the accumulated treasures of Jewish mystical lore. Surely in a different age and place these mystical enthusiasts would have remained out of the mainstream. Only in the given conditions of their environment were they able to exercise such a tremendous influence and create a new religious movement. However, once the movement was called into existence, the relation between leader and follower underwent a change, and the leader personified to a considerable extent in his beliefs and actions the peculiar popular characteristics of his believers. Leaders and communities fused together and through their concerted efforts gave rise to different variants of chasiduth.

With the passage of the "Heroic Period" (1760-1815) and the cessation of the struggle between the chasidim and their opponents (*mithnagdim*), the dynamic force of the movement exhausted itself. There arose constant divisions within the ranks, and the tzaddikim often became more interested in exploiting their power and extending their influence than in the spiritual values of chasiduth. The term "chasid" no longer carried any distinctive meaning, and had to be modified with an adjective, such as "Lubavitcher" or "Sadigorer," which meant a partisan of the Rebbe of Lubavitch or the Rebbe of Sadigora. The office of the tzaddik became hereditary, and in some cases the "territory" of a tzaddik was parceled out to all his children. After the death of Rabbi Mordecai of Chernobyl (1837), his "empire" was divided among his eight sons. Constant quarrels and rivalries marred the relationship between the various warring dynasties of tzaddikim and their passionate chasidim.

With the popular acceptance of the movement and its settling down to the day-to-day conduct of its affairs, the regional differences became more apparent. In Volhynia and Podolia, where chasiduth had originated, and in the adjoining provinces of the Ukraine and Rumania, tzaddikim reigned supreme. The Besht's grandson, Rabbi Baruch of Tulchin, who occupied his grandfather's "throne," was more influential in the future conduct of tzaddikim than his renowned grandfather. He was the first tzaddik to wax rich on the gifts of his chasidim, build himself a palace, and live after the manner of Polish magnates and church dignitaries. He even maintained a court fool, Herschel Ostropoler, the famous teller of popular folk stories and anecdotes. This grandson of the Besht is reported to have said, perhaps facetiously, that God placed in the tzaddik's heart a desire for money, which makes him join himself to the children of Israel and lift up their prayers. He claimed to have been told by Rabbi Shimon ben Yochai, who lived almost two thousand years previously, that he was a righteous tzaddik. Thus, Rabbi Baruch was distinguished from the other contemporary tzaddikim who, according to him, did not know how to worship God in the right manner.

Rabbi Baruch's court was soon overshadowed by that of Rabbi Israel of Rizhin, the greatgrandson of the Great Maggid. These two set the tone for many tzaddikim of Ukrainian chasiduth. They were mainly "practitioners" and miracle workers. Their exalted position rested entirely on the claim that they were intermediaries between God and the children of Israel.

This type of tzaddik-worship, accepted eagerly as genuine religious teaching and behavior by the illiterate and unsophisticated village Jews of the Ukraine and Rumania, was completely out of line with the feelings of the Jews of the older and more settled communities to the north. Talmudic learning prevailed there in much wider circles, and Kabbalic teaching did not make such inroads into the people's minds as it did in the provinces near the Turkish border. Under the influence of the venerated Rabbi Elijah of Wilno (1720-1797), rabbinism was more vigorous and Talmudic learning more widely diffused. Here chasiduth had to engage in a bitter struggle for its very existence, and be defined in terms acceptable to the Talmudic scholar. The exponent of this interpretation of chasiduth was Rabbi Shneur Zalman of Liadi (later of Lubavitch) (1747-1813), who succeeded in creating an impressive system of thought, known by the name "Chabad," the Hebrew initials for "Wisdom, Reason, Knowledge."

In keeping within the tradition of Jewish mysticism, Rabbi

Shneur Zalman was concerned with the relation of God to the world. Creation is continuous, for the power of God permeates all His creatures, animate and inanimate alike. His presence is everywhere, and we must learn to penetrate into the inner essence of things, beyond the conventional cover of orderliness, in order to comprehend this inner Divine Light. The human soul emanates from God, and it is concerned with achieving a knowledge of Him and His manifestations. An understanding of God must induce man to fear and to love Him with enthusiasm and deep emotion.

Fear of God should not come from the fear of punishment, but rather from an intelligent understanding of the beauty and marvels of creation. "I have no need for Thy promise of heaven. Thee alone I need, and for Thee alone I yearn, to be absorbed in Thy Holy Being."[6] Contemplative understanding of religion takes prominence over more enthusiastic displays of religious feeling. Wisdom, Reason, and Knowledge are the greatest attainments of human life, and they can be achieved only by those who have comprehended the mysteries of the Torah.

Prayer is the foundation and essence of the Torah and the channel through which the Divine blessings may be diverted to earth. God listens to everybody's prayer, if it is genuine; and Rabbi Shneur Zalman remonstrated with his followers to pray to God personally for the fulfillment of their needs. He even refused to bear the title "tzaddik" and chose instead that of rabbi. He rejected the concept of the tzaddik as mediator between God and man, considering it foreign to Jewish thought and practice. Himself he regarded as a teacher and instructor of the people in the knowledge of Torah. He insisted that people come to him to learn his message, and not for help in things material.

The third school of chasiduth developed in the central Polish areas, or as it was known for a long time, Congressional Poland. Chasiduth came to this territory after it had already passed its heroic period and shifted into a cult of tzaddikim. And this was the form of chasiduth that best suited the needs of the helpless and superstitious masses during the partition of Poland and the ceaseless wars that followed them. The message of the new teachings reached the central provinces of Poland from the court of Rabbi Elimelech of Lizensk. During the four decades that elapsed from his death (1778) until the demise of the first two great Polish tzaddikim (1815), Rabbi Israel, the Maggid of Kozenitz, and Rabbi Jacob Isaac, the Seer of Lublin, the chasidic conquest of the country was almost completed.

Both these men were famous as wonder workers, and Jews from all over the country came to them for advice and blessings. In 1808 the Polish government of the Warsaw Duchy proclaimed compulsory military service for Jews and also prohibited them from participating in the liquor trade. These two decrees rocked the foundations of the established Jewish economy and way of life, and multitudes flocked to the tzaddikim for help. The Maggid of Kozenitz assured his chasidim that "The tzaddikim teach God Almighty how to conduct Himself and how to treat His children, to abrogate unfavorable decrees, to renew the good ones, and to bring salvation and consolation."

Rabbi Jacob Isaac, the Seer of Lubin, was believed able to read a man's mind just by looking at him with his penetrating eyes. He could recognize a person's character and activities just by reading the handwriting on the notes of request handed to him. He was famous for his scholarship and bemoaned the fact that he was unable to study Torah because all his time was taken up by listening to the troubles and needs of his people. However, he regarded as his prime duty "to look also downward at this world and take into consideration Israel's livelihood, that no material needs shall be wanting."[7]

Only when the material wants of Israel will be satisfied will their hearts turn to love God and fear Him. Then will they be in a position to rejoice in His service and pray to Him with an overflowing heart. The Seer himself was famous for his ecstatic prayer; his hands, legs, and all his limbs swayed and trembled, and quite often he fell into a trance that lasted for hours. His chasidim said that the spirit of God rested on him and he saw visions like a prophet. "Whoever came to Lublin had the feeling that he was entering the Land of Israel; the yard of his house of study was like Jerusalem, his house of study like the Mount of the Temple, his dwelling place the Temple itself; and the study of the Seer — the Holy of Holies, and the Divine Presence talked through him."[8]

However, the intellectual atmosphere surrounding the court of the tzaddik in Poland was different than that in the Ukraine. The masses, in spite of their credulity and superstition, respected learning, and aspired that their children would receive a thorough Talmudic grounding. These Jews lived mostly in small towns and not in scattered peasant villages — not like Jews in the provinces bordering on the southeastern frontier. The tzaddikim themselves were men of learning and liked to surround themselves with scholars. An air of veneration for learning, "the fragrance of Torah," pervaded the entire social climate of Polish Jewry — even in its early expression of chasiduth. Although the first two leaders of Polish chasiduth resembled in their conduct their Ukrainian and Podolian counterparts, a change was bound to come.

Many of the young Polish Talmud students were deeply

affected by the warmth and religiosity of chasidic teachings. Through their contact with chasiduth, their legalistic-Talmudic discussions gained a new dimension of depth. Their knowledge became converted into a glowing, living faith. They desired a scholarly kind of chasiduth that would satisfy their intellectual needs. They wanted to discuss and analyze chasiduth as they analyzed and discussed fine points in the Talmud. Their hearts were set upon a tzaddik who would be a guide and a mentor in these studies, as the head of a Talmudic academy was. They were repelled by the masses' belief in the miracle-working tzaddik and his claims to supernatural powers. They desired a more serious and more learned chasidic message. "The Jew of Peshischa," the great disciple of the Seer, served as a rallying point for this opposition. He taught a new kind of chasiduth, which was extended by his disciples Rabbi Simcha Bunim of Peshischa and Rabbi Menachem Mendel of Kotzk. Through the influence of these three men the Polish school of chasiduth began its ascent to maturity.

Chapter 3 — Notes

1. Horodetzky, S. A., *HaChasiduth VeHaChasidim*, v. 1, p. 55, Chapter Three
2. Dubnow, *Toldot HaChasiduth*, p. 82
3. Minkin, *l. c.*, p. 158
4. Dubnow, *l. c.*, p. 91
5. Dubnow, *l. c.*, pp. 180-183
6. Minkin, *l. c.*, p. 215; also Zeitlin, Hillel, *Araynifir in Chasiduth un der Veg fun Chabad*, p. 54 ff.
7. Finkelstein, Leo, *Megillat Polin*, p. 138
8. Rabinovitz, H. M., *Rabbi Yaakov Yitzchak Mi'Peshischa*, p. 42

Chapter 4

The Peshischa System

Peshischa was the forerunner of Kotzk, and the spiritual biography of Rabbi Menachem Mendel of Kotzk was tied up with the personality of Rabbi Jacob Isaac of Peshischa, known commonly as *HaYehudi HaKadosh* ("The Holy Jew"), or the Jew of Peshischa (1776-1814). A scion of a family of scholars, Rabbi Jacob Isaac was early in his life attracted to the chasidic movement. His Talmudic knowledge was remarkable and his capacity for study boundless. He used to tell that his scholarship was due to a neighbor of his, a blacksmith; when he went to sleep, he heard the blows of the blacksmith's hammer. He thought that it did not behoove a servant of God to retire, if a simple blacksmith could still go on working. So he returned to his tome of the Talmud and studied it in a loud chant. When the blacksmith heard the young man's voice, he was sure that it was still early and he continued with his work; so did the student with his Talmud. The same went on in the morning. The first blow of the blacksmith's hammer brought him back to his studies; in such a way he became a Talmudic scholar of renown.

In his search for deeper meaning, the Talmudic student soon became a savant of the Kabbala. He spent nights in solitary reflection, and his prayers became rapturous and exalted. Every waking moment of his life was dedicated to the service of God and the elevation of the soul. His aim was moral perfection through the study of Torah, through prayer, and through pious deeds.

A number of years went by, and Rabbi Jacob Isaac became aware that he had achieved a higher "level" of existence. It also dawned on him that there existed a physical limit to the perfectibility of man. Even though his soul desired to rise to even higher spheres and seek union with eternity, his human flesh was unable to follow these yearnings. Man can achieve godliness only within the scope allowed by his humanity, and this limitation stems from God Himself. Rabbi Jacob Isaac realized that further self-denial and affliction would bring his death, and God surely did not want the righteous ones to die. God takes delight in their devotion and is anxious for their prayers. Man must, therefore, live out his allotted number of years and serve God to the best of his ability. However, how could he be assured that his way of serving God was the right one? The rabbi felt the need for a critical evaluation of his ideas and deeds by someone in authority. He realized that he must seek the company and advice of a teacher who could guide him. This state of mind brought him to the Seer of Lublin.

In Lublin, the newly converted chasid was accepted with open arms. The Seer was eager to surround himself with men of learning, and desired to give his popular brand of chasiduth a dimension of depth and piety. "Love of Israel" was the most cherished moral value in Lublin. However, in its practical application "love for Israel" meant that the tzaddik's entire day was taken up with the everyday needs and misfortunes of his manifold petitioners, and very little time was left for delving into the depths of chasidic theory. The function of developing a chasidic philosophy, and teaching it to the scholarly devotees, was delegated to Rabbi Jacob Isaac. He soon became the central figure of the "holy society" of scholars of the Seer's court. The young Talmudic scholars, motivated by a burning desire to live as Jews on a higher level of emotional and moral intensity, were directed by the Seer to seek Rabbi Jacob Isaac's company. Everybody capable and willing to dedicate himself to serious study and profound thinking was accepted by this "holy society."

As both men, the Seer and his disciple, bore the name Jacob Isaac, the disciple was referred to as "The Holy Jew," or just "The Jew." Chasidic tradition tells us that the prime ambition of "The Jew" was to be a Jew. It was not enough that our ancestors once accepted the Torah at Mt. Sinai; to him the receiving of the Torah was a continuous, never-ending process. Every moment of his life, he aspired to be conscious of his Jewishness, to penetrate into the depth of its meaning, and to live up to its precepts.

To be a Jew was not something that could be given as a gift or gained by proxy, through the prayer of the tzaddik. A Jew has to struggle to be a Jew. The greatest enemy of a Jew is his body and bodily temptations. While satisfying his bodily needs, the Jew is liable to forget for awhile his Creator, and the real meaning of life, which is moral betterment.

Once, after finishing his protracted prayers, "The Jew" sat down to his meal, and it seemed to him that he enjoyed his bread and soup. He could not forgive himself the sin of having taken pleasure in the good things of this world, for the sake of enjoyment, and not for the distinct purpose of serving God. He prayed to God for punishment for this transgression, and soon fell to the floor in convulsions of pain. When his disciples reminded him that the time for the evening prayer had arrived, he rose and

48

announced that he had already taken revenge upon his greatest enemy, his body; he was now ready to serve God with a pure heart.[1]

It was impossible for a man of such trend of mind to dwell together with the Seer for a prolonged period. In spite of all the good intentions of the Seer and his unquestionable personal piety and integrity, the atmosphere around him was charged with veneration for his great power of performing miracles for the poor and needy. In the eyes of "The Jew" this was a degeneration of chasiduth and a profanation of its sublime message. To "The Jew," chasiduth was the quintessence of Judaism; genuine religion should be concerned with the spiritual and moral needs of men and with their strivings for perfection and unity with God. His aim was to effect a renaissance of chasiduth that would restore it to its original purity. This ambition of regenerating chasiduth and raising it to ever-higher levels of spirituality would hence become the moving power behind the Peshischa system and its three great spokesmen: "The Holy Jew," Rabbi Simcha Bunim, and — above all — Rabbi Menachem Mendel of Kotzk.

The "holy society" of Talmudic scholars at the court of the tzaddik of Lublin shared the opinions of "The Jew," and its members encouraged him to found his own school of chasiduth. Moving to Peshischa, they established their headquarters there. Nevertheless, "The Jew" did not regard this move as a secession and breakaway from the Seer. In spite of all the intrigues and ill will that were created between these two seats of chasiduth, "The Jew" continued his annual pilgrimages to the Seer and regarded his own school as an offshoot of the Lublin system.

According to "The Jew," Lublin was the "king's highway" to chasiduth for all of Israel, while Peshischa was for the chosen few with the courage and ability to reach beyond the commonplace. "The Jew" was very particular in admitting new adherents to his circle of disciples. His aim was to gather around himself young men of high scholastic achievement, whose main purpose in life was spiritual and moral self-perfection. He did not regard himself as a tzaddik possessed of supernatural powers in the accepted chasidic way. Rather, he was a guide and a senior colleague to a circle of friends engaged in the study of Torah and concerned with the most rigorous fulfillment of its commandments. To "The Jew," the verse "Thou shalt surely release it with him" (Exodus 23:5) meant that the chasid must help his tzaddik guide him on the path of righteousness. Only when the chasid himself will be preoccupied with his own elevation, and works hard towards self-improvement, will the tzaddik be able to help the chasid achieve the goals that the latter has set for himself.

To "The Jew," the commandment "Love thy neighbor as thyself" (Leviticus 19:18) did not mean that one should love all his fellow Jews in the same way. Surely this was not the intent of the Torah, because man should love the righteous more than the wicked. The emphasis should be on the words "as thyself." Just as a man does not love all the limbs of his body in the same way, attaching more importance to the heart and head than to the hands or lips, so should every man be loved and appreciated according to his value.

The keynote of "The Jew's" concept of chasiduth was the old Talmudic dictum: "The ignoramus is not a chasid" (Aboth 2:6). The chasid himself, concerned with achieving the highest goals of Jewish learning and living, is a partner with the tzaddik in forming the essence of chasiduth. In contradistinction to the prevailing pattern developed by the Seer, "The Jew's" brand of chasiduth stressed the following four points:

1. Talmudic learning as the basic requirement for the chasidic way of life.
2. Opposition to the superficiality of chasidic folkways and the substitution of tzaddik-worship for Torah study.
3. Resistance to the wonder-workings of the tzaddik.
4. Prayer as the most sublime form of worship, and the freedom of the individual to choose his own time and mode of prayer.

"The Jew's" purpose in placing the emphasis of chasiduth on Torah-learning was not to foster a critical-analytical attitude of free inquiry among his followers, but to intensify their inner religiosity and deepen their moral sensitivity. "Truth is the seal of the Holy One Blessed Be His Name" (Shabbath 55), and all human thought and behavior should be saturated with this Divine quality of truth. The impregnation of the head and heart with truth means the complete elimination of pride and selfishness, not only in deed and conversation but also in thought and self-evaluation. A chasid should remain humble, even when he knows that he has achieved the highest possible level of self-improvement. "After having climbed the highest levels of understanding and perception, the chasid should remain a simple Jew."[2]

The following story should exemplify well the concept of chasiduth held by "The Jew." Rabbi Isaac Meir, the future tzaddik of Ger, once asked Rabbi Simcha Bunim, who was considered the most outstanding disciple of "The Jew": What did he regard as the most fundamental principle of Judaism? To this Rabbi Simcha Bunim replied: "Lift up your eyes on high and see, who hath created these?" (Isaiah 40:26). However, "The Jew" did not agree with this answer and stated that there was no need for basing the teachings of Judaism on creation and general philosophical considerations. To his mind, the basic teaching of the Torah was contained in the First Commandment: "I am the Lord, thy God, who brought thee out of the land of Egypt, out of the house of bondage" (Exodus 20:2). The existence of God, as manifested in the unique historic experiences of Israel, expressed the substance of "The Jew's" faith.[3]

The teachings of "The Holy Jew" and the entire Peshischa brand of chasiduth provoked a heated controversy. The Seer of Lublin and all the other tzaddikim resented his belittling the role of miracles, and rightly saw in this a challenge to their authority. However, much more opposition was evoked by his theory that man should pray when he was emotionally predisposed to it, disregarding the limitations of time set for prayer by the Jewish codes of law. All the conservative elements in Judaism saw in this a dangerous breach of tradition, and instigated a campaign of slander and vilification against the Peshischa chasidim.

However, all the defamation and persecution could not stem the progress of the Peshischa system. Its message exerted a magical pull on many of the young Talmudic scholars, who saw in Peshischa the fulfillment of their innermost cravings for a life of meaning. "The Jew" was not privileged to witness the popular acceptance of the movement initiated by him. His ascetic practices ruined his health and he succumbed at the age of forty-eight. Contrary to chasidic practice, his successor was not his son, but his most promising disciple, the aforementioned Rabbi Simcha Bunim.

Chasidic tradition relates that when "The Jew" died his orphaned chasidim came to Rabbi Simcha Bunim and asked him who should become tzaddik in place of the deceased master. Instead of giving an answer, Rabbi Simcha Bunim told them the following allegory:

A shepherd once fell asleep at noon and slept until midnight, leaving his flock to graze unattended. When he woke up, he became frightened and worried about the welfare of his flock. Slowly he rose from his bed of grass, looked around, and saw above him the pure heavens, the shining noon, and the twinkling stars in their divine splendor. The air was fragrant and the entire flock was standing near a stream of water rippling pleasantly and quietly in the still of the night.

From the shepherd's heart burst forth a prayer of thanksgiving and he said: "Oh, my Father in heaven, what shall I give Thee in exchange for Your kindness? How may I, a poor shepherd, thank Thee? Only by vowing that from this day hence I shall guard Your flock like the apple of my eye."

If you will find such a faithful shepherd, accept him as your master.

When the chasidim heard this allegory, they rose from their places and seated Rabbi Simcha Bunim on the chair of his late teacher.

Rabbi Simcha Bunim (1765-1827) was an unusual man to occupy the seat of a chasidic tzaddik. For a number of years he served as business agent for the famous Bergson family of Warsaw. A frequent visitor to the German commercial cities of Danzig and Leipzig, he spoke Polish and German, attended theaters, and was supposedly good at playing cards with the businessmen whose houses he visited. After retiring from the Bergson concern, he took up the study of pharmacy, passed the required examinations before the medical board of Lvov, and received the degree of "qualified pharmacist." All this was quite unusual for an Orthodox Jew at the time. He made a comfortable living with his pharmacy in Peshischa, which was patronized by the Polish nobility from the surrounding countryside and by the local population. This pharmacist was also a Talmudic scholar of renown and an adherent of the Seer of Lublin, who was supposed to have promised to bestow upon him "the holy spirit from the sphere of spirituality." Later on he followed "The Holy Jew" and soon he became his most outstanding disciple.

Though he was no less determined than his master to restore chasiduth to its pristine purity, Rabbi Simcha Bunim was a completely different type of man. His most notable character trait was not the mystical longing for union with God, as was the case with "The Holy Jew," but the philosopher's quietude of mind and striving for intellectual and moral perfection. He explained the difference between the Lublin and Peshischa schools of chasiduth in the following way: "The Seer of Lublin became a tzaddik with the verse 'He hath neither despised nor abhorred the affliction of the poor' (Psalms 22:25); and I with the verse 'Say unto wisdom, thou art my sister' (Proverbs 7:4). The Talmud teaches, 'There is no poor but in knowledge.' "[4]

The pharmacist-turned-tzaddik soon became the object of sneer and ridicule among the opposing chasidic circles. Rabbi Meir of Apta pointedly asked if Rabbi Simcha Bunim had reached his high level of spirituality at the fair of Danzig, in the German theaters, or among his jars of chemicals. When told about it, Rabbi Simcha Bunim was neither angered nor perturbed by this pious dig, but replied calmly: "The contemporary tzaddikim do not know why one sins and in what way he sins; therefore, they are ignorant of the cure. However, I know what causes men to sin, and I know also how to effect the necessary remedies."[5]

This derision of Peshischa soon turned into a loud outcry of indignation, when Rabbi Simcha Bunim's deviations from the accepted path of East European Orthodoxy became known. He encouraged his chasidim to study the writings of the medieval Spanish philosophers, and personally introduced the study of Saadia, Yehuda Halevi, Maimonides, and Yedaiah Hapnini. He aspired to republish the books of Maimonides in a popular edition with brief notes of commentary. One of his followers took up this idea and began to publish chapters from the *Code of Maimonides* in a cheap edition.[6] Rabbi Simcha Bunim praised Abraham Ibn Ezra's commentary to the Bible, which was known to contain highly critical remarks as to the authorship of some chapters in the Pentateuch. This raised the ire of all the Orthodox, *mithnagdim* and chasidim alike.

As indicated before, the verse "Lift up your eyes on high and see who hath created these" (Isaiah 40:26) played a very important part in the system of thought evolved by Rabbi Simcha Bunim. To worship God properly, one has to understand the manifestation of Divine intelligence in nature and its magnificent regularity and orderliness. Nature was to Rabbi Simcha Bunim the greatest miracle, and the proper understanding of its harmony and appreciation of its beauty inspired awe and confidence in the workings of God. He doubted the wisdom of the people who required miracles in order to experience the guiding hand of God. "Signs and miracles in the land of the ignorant" (Psalms 105:27) was his often repeated saying.[7] On his scale of values he assigned a greater importance to the belief that comes from understanding and examination; he deprecated the simple faith that stems from naivete.

To these two principles, Torah study and open-minded investigation, Rabbi Simcha Bunim added a third one: the will that creates the desire for study and generates the feeling conducive to worship of God. Knowledge and will, reason and emotion — all these should be merged and intermingled when man fulfills God's commandments. Observance and prayer demand an attitude of exaltation and comprehension. The Peshischa chasidim rejected mere mechanical prayer and observance; they stressed, instead, prior preparation in order to be in the right frame of mind for prayer. They became known for their long delays and special preparations before prayer.

And there were still some other deviations from tradition. On Rosh Hashana the Peshischa chasidim used to get up at sunrise and start with their devotions. When all the other Jews went to their houses of worship for prayer, they found the Peshischa chasidim preoccupied with the study of Talmud or some philosophical text. The Peshischa chasidim constantly emphasized their disapproval of accepted folk customs, if they are performed mechanically without previous inner spiritual preparation.

Good deeds and acts of piety and charity should be performed quietly and in concealment, in order to avoid publicity and the false feeling of pride, according to the teachings of Peshischa. Very often Rabbi Simcha Bunim's chasidim refused to participate in communal prayer sessions and charity campaigns, preferring instead to perform all these religious duties far away from the public eye. All this provoked a campaign of vilification against Rabbi Simcha Bunim and all the Peshischa chasidim. At one point, during a famous wedding in Ostila, when close to two hundred Polish rabbis and tzaddikim came together, the Peshischa chasidim were spared the impending proclamation of excommunication only by a stroke of sheer luck.[8]

Together with the admiration for nature came a different outlook on the role of the human body. Rabbi Simcha Bunim neither agreed with his master's teaching, "My body is my greatest enemy," nor condoned a moderate enjoyment of the good things in life. He emphasized personal hygiene, external cleanliness, and orderly appearance in dress. His chasidim were spic-and-span. The beard and earlocks were washed and combed, and the clothing they wore was expected to be spotless.

Besides this personal cleanliness, the chasidim of Peshischa could be recognized by their walk and customs. They did not bow their heads, but walked straight and erect. Man must enjoy life. This is the intent of the Creator, and obedience to it leads to a better understanding of God and His ways. Peshischa chasidim walked during the spring days in the fields and forests to enjoy the splendor of nature. They loved to hear the sound of music, and sang melodious tunes at their gatherings. They saw in nature's beauty and soft echoes the power of the Creator, and desired to share in His secret.

The two aforementioned distinctive features of Rabbi Simcha Bunim's personality — his indulgence in philosophic reflection and his aesthetic outlook — made his view of the *haskala* movement different from that of all his chasidic contemporaries. Surely, he had no sympathy for the *maskilim*'s laxity of religious observance or their desire to secularize Jewish life. However, the propensity of the *haskala* followers to reexamine critically all the foundations of Jewish belief and foster open-mindedness was not foreign to him at all. His was a Torah-centered *haskala,* and he possessed an ardor for examining Jewish values through the means, standards, and concepts developed by medieval Jewish philosophy. He did not reject altogether the modern world. He was ready to accommodate himself externally to the demands of modern life, but denied its influence on the Jewish way of thought. For a time he believed that through fostering the works of the Spanish-Jewish enlightenment he would succeed in stemming the tide of the secular *haskala* of his day. Though he was respected by some of the *haskala* writers, they were not deterred from following their own course of action.

In all aspects of religious life and ethical behavior, Rabbi Simcha Bunim was a faithful follower of his deceased master. He insisted on the uncompromising search for truth in thought, word, and action. To him, truth should permeate the totality of religious and practical life. Any word or deed that was not a true expression of inner cravings and convictions was to him a falsehood, or a conventional lie at best. He had only contempt for the man who worshiped God and performed the religious duties only out of habit or a desire to conform. The keyword to his entire system of chasiduth was "inwardness."

Rabbi Menachem Mendel, the future tzaddik of Kotzk, grew up in this atmosphere of unending search for truth and demand for inner consistency between thought, belief, and action. From the personalities of the two great masters of Peshischa, "The Holy Jew" and Rabbi Simcha Bunim, he inherited his great passion for a renaissance of chasiduth and moral perfection. It was his allotted function in life to bring the teachings of his predecessors to their logical conclusion and give them wide acclaim. The story of his rise to prominence and subsequent downfall gives a splendid illustration to all that was inherently great and tragic in the chasidic movement.

Chapter 4 — Notes

The factual material contained in this chapter is based primarily upon the two excellent monographs written by Zvi Meir Rabinovitz: *Rabbi Yaakov Yitzchak Mi'Peshischa, HaYehudi HaKadosh, Zmano, Chayav, Ve'Torato,* and *Rabbi Simcha Bunim Mi'Peshischa, Chayav Ve'Torato.*

1. Steinman, Eliezer, *Be'er HaChasidut, Admorey Polin,* p. 82

2. Rabinovitz, Zvi Meir, *Rabbi Yaakov Yitzchak Mi'Peshischa,* p. 89
3. Rabinovitz, Zvi Meir, *Rabbi Simcha Bunim Mi'Peshischa,* p. 49
4. Ibid., *1. c.,* p. 24
5. *Ramataim Tzofim,* p. 41
6. Rabinovitz, *l. c.,* p. 46
7. Rabinovitz, *l. c.,* p. 53
8. Rabinovitz, *1. c.,* p. 28. A nice narrative description of this event is to be found in the first chapter of Menashe Unger's *Fun Peshischa bis Kotzk.*

Chapter 5

His Lublin and Peshischa Origins

Menachem Mendel, whose family name was Morgenstern, and who was known in the chasidic world as Rabbi Menachem Mendel of Kotzk, was born around 1788 in the town of Guryea, in the district of Lublin.

His father, Reb Leibush, belonged to a poor and insignificant family.[1] A window repairman, he used to cruise around in the neighboring villages, a load of window glass on his shoulders, and repair damaged windows. He is known to have been an authoritarian who demanded from his children strict obedience, and who insisted that they grow up to be exemplary people. Nothing short of perfection satisfied him.[2] Menachem Mendel, his youngest son, was endowed with a brilliant mind. He studied the Torah day and night, and became expert in the Talmud and Codes. He knew the Talmud by heart.

The future Rabbi of Kotzk has been described as a self-assured, serious-minded, lonely boy, with apparent mystical tendencies. Once, when he disagreed with his teacher about the exact meaning of a Biblical passage, he is quoted as having remarked: "Do not argue with me; I remember that I stood on Mount Sinai and heard God saying, 'I am the Lord your God.'"[3] A second story relates that once, on Lag B'Omer, when all the school children went on a hike and played with bow and arrow, they suddenly discovered that Menachem Mendel had disappeared. After a search, they found him lying on the ground and singing, in a whining voice, "My heart and flesh sing to the living God" (Psalms 84:3).[4]

This boy possessed unusual zest and a rare genius for study. His Talmud teacher was a remarkable person, who exerted a great influence on the boy's character. This teacher, over-critical and exact, did not speak much, but every one of his words was pointed and meaningful. From his youthful students he demanded insight and a complete understanding of the text, inviting short and concise answers.[5] Menachem Mendel soon gained a reputation as an outstanding student who had a complete mastery of the Talmud. He quoted entire volumes verbatim, along with the commentaries and marginal remarks. He derived pleasure from the exactness and logic involved in the study of the Talmud. In his latter years he used to say, "A page of Gemara purifies like a ritual bath."[6]

The future Rabbi of Kotzk also had some secular education. After the first partition of Poland (1772), the town of Guryea was incorporated into the Austrian monarchy. According to a law promulgated by the Emperor Josef II, no Jewish boy was allowed to marry unless he passed an exam in the knowledge of German and learned a trade. According to chasidic tradition, Menachem Mendel spent some time in the provincial capital of Lvov, where he studied German and also learned to be an apothecary. It is not easy to determine whether this exposure to secular learning had any influence on the make-up of his mind and ways of thinking. The chasidic story points out that he was forced to learn German but "took special care that it did no harm to him."[7]

His parents, ardent *mithnagdim*, were concerned that he should not come under the influence of the "sect." Due to their efforts, he was in his youth an opponent to chasiduth and attracted greatly to the Wilno Gaon. The good name of the young scholar soon reached the courts of the chasidic leaders, many of whom wanted to draw him to their side and win him as a follower.

Although Menachem Mendel was educated as a *mithnaged,* and was fond of the Talmud and its specific ways of reasoning, the recourse to logic alone did not satisfy his emotional cravings. The lonely boy yearned for companionship and emotional satisfaction. His imagination must have been stirred by stories of the great chasidic rebbes and their closeness to the heavenly sources of all wisdom and knowledge. It was in keeping with the times for young and promising men to throw their lot with that of the growing chasidic movement. This might have been an expression of rebellion against authoritarian parents and the repressive environment. The hilarity of the chasidic gatherings, their reputation for good fellowship and keen sense of community, together with the stark opposition towards them from the elders, attracted to chasiduth many young men who searched for a life of meaning and sociability.

The young Menachem Mendel of Guryea followed this trend of the times. To him, life was the search for meaning and truth. We know that he was never seriously preoccupied with the everyday concerns of mortals, like making a living and providing for a family. His only lifelong occupation was study, prayer, and understanding of God and His ways. In his thinking he was logical and critical, as it behooved a student of the Talmud. However, the mystical urgings within him and the determination of a dissatisfied truth-seeker brought him into the chasidic camp.

The chasidic legend gives the Seer of Lublin the credit for winning over this unusual young man. The Seer, whose far-seeing eyes missed nothing, noted this rising star. He told a teacher of Guryea that in his city "flickers a holy spark" that was worthy of attention. The Seer wanted Menachem Mendel brought to him. From that time on, the teacher observed the activities of his fellow townsmen — but in vain, for he could not find that spark. In desperation, the teacher decided to sleep in the house of study and there solve the mystery. At midnight, young Menachem Mendel entered alone, and began to study Talmud with great enthusiasm and devotion. The teacher then understood that this was the youth the tzaddik had referred to; but, to be completely sure, he came to the house of study on several more nights, and on every occasion found the boy studying with vigor and affection "which penetrated the heavens." When the teacher was certain that Menachem Mendel was the secret one referred to by the Seer, he emerged from his hiding place and told the lad about his purpose in coming to him. At the beginning, Menachem Mendel attempted to discourage him, but this made the teacher even more certain. Finally, Menachem Mendel yielded and journeyed with him to Lublin.[8]

Menachem Mendel's first encounter with a real chasidic leader was symptomatic of the entire course of his future life. He remained critical and dissatisfied. It was relatively easy to answer his reprimanding father, who attempted to bring him back home from Lublin, citing the verse: "This is my God and I will glorify Him, my father's God and I will exalt Him" (Exodus 15:2). First comes "This is my God" — I have to find my own God and worship Him according to my own ways and understanding; and only later on may I consider "my father's God."[9] It was much more difficult for him to decide for himself whether his God was a God who could be comprehended logically, or perceived mystically. Anyhow, the kind of mysticism combined with "tzaddik-worship" that he found in Lublin was not to his liking. Menachem Mendel was cut of another grain and not ready to accept unhesitatingly all the miraculous stories told by the admiring chasidim about their rebbe. He must have been repulsed by all that he saw and heard at the capital of Polish chasiduth. He had a temperamental nature, and so we have a right to assume that he voiced his opinions publicly. Ultimately, this caused a rift with the Seer and Menachem Mendel left Lublin.

Years later, Rabbi Menachem Mendel told his son-in-law, Rabbi Abraham of Sochatzev, that upon his arrival at Lublin he was bestowed the rare honor of being invited to pray with the Seer. It took him many years of labor to erase from his heart the feelings of pride and self-importance aroused by this incident.[10]

The Seer noticed that Menachem Mendel was critical of his teachings and conduct, and asked him once: "Tell me, Menachem Mendel, why did you come here? Did you come only to buy a pocket knife?"

And Menachem Mendel retorted: "I surely did not come to see the Divine Spirit, and I refuse to be captivated by it."

Before the final parting of their ways, the Seer was reported to issue the following warning to his rebellious disciple: "Your way leads to gloom; leave it, because I cannot foresee success for you."[11] These words, in retrospect, have an ominous ring.

Menachem Mendel pursued the logical implications of his first choice. He did not repudiate chasiduth altogether, but followed the road leading to a synthesis between the Jewish tradition of scholarship, which was deeply ingrained in his make-up, and the mystical stirrings set on foot by chasidic teachings, which so thoroughly affected his heart. He was attracted to Peshischa, the residence of "The Jew," in whom he expected to find a kindred spirit sympathetic to his aspirations and motives.

"The Jew" was already a rival to the Seer, though an open break between the two had not yet come. Menachem Mendel left Lublin without his master's permission, which was contrary to chasidic custom. Legend has it, therefore, that all the way to Peshischa he was ailing and arrived very sick. "The Jew" knew at once that this young man must have left his rebbe without bidding him farewell. He advised Menachem Mendel to return and ask for his master's blessing. However, Menachem Mendel refused categorically to accept this advice, announcing that he was not sorry for what he had done. "If he has such strong determination, then he will get well," the rabbi of Peshischa was reported to say. Soon after, Menachem Mendel recovered and became one of the pillars of the Peshischa system.[12]

When the Seer once asked "The Jew" if he had a follower worthy of notice, the latter replied that in Menachem Mendel he had such a disciple. This distinction assured Menachem Mendel that he was on the right path. He was reported to have made the following remark: "Until then I did not want [to be a chasid], but from that hour on I was instilled with a constant desire to accept the yoke of Heavenly Kingdom."[13]

It was in Peshischa that Rabbi Menachem Mendel, the future revolutionary, found peace of mind and spiritual satisfaction. Here he found chasidim who were mainly concerned with self-betterment and living on a higher intellectual and moral level. Here they were cured from the "wonder" stupor that predominated in Lublin. In Peshischa his character took form, and his ideas crystallized. Here developed his desire for revolution and innovation, and he began to see clearly his way in life.

Menachem Mendel reached spiritual maturity during the times of Rabbi Simcha Bunim, who followed "The Jew." Here was a man whom he could understand and admire. However, it would be wrong to assume that Menachem Mendel accepted everything that his rabbis taught and did. He was not a "chasid," an admiring and unthinking follower, as the term was then understood. He was rather a discriminating and critical eclectic, who took even from his most admired teachers only what suited him. He felt neither humble nor submissive in the presence of great minds and outstanding personalities. He could never submerge himself and be carried away by a movement or system. Forever critical and self-conscious, he was "a chasid who was at root a *mithnaged.*"[14] In later years, as Rabbi of Kotzk, he gave the term "chasid" a number of different definitions, one of which was: "A man who ponders over his every word and deed and asks himself: What do I want to achieve through them?"[15]

Though Menachem Mendel greatly admired "The Jew," this did not stop him from disagreeing with some of the latter's actions. "The Rabbi of Peshischa," he said, "always fulfilled the commandment: 'thou shalt surely help him out' (Exodus 23:5), and he used to help everybody to reach ever higher levels. I, however, would like to see every individual rise through his own efforts."[16] Even a rabbi should not interfere in the relationship between man and God. It is every man's duty to rise constantly to an ever-higher comprehension of the Divine, and this cannot be done through an intermediary.

Rabbi Simcha Bunim was known to be an aesthetician, who took meticulous care of his dress and outer appearance. To

Menachem Mendel, this was non-essential. He poked fun at the Peshischa chasidim who looked like angels for a time and later resembled beggars. "Are these really worthy of redemption?" He himself held in utter disregard all forms of good behavior and attachment to material things. At the age of fourteen he was married and received a dowry of a thousand gold pieces. When he came to Peshischa he distributed all his money among his poor friends; even his handsome cloak, a gift from his father-in-law, he gave to the chasidim to pawn for cake and whiskey. He immediately clothed himself in tattered rags, in contrast to the spic-and-span chasidim of Rabbi Simcha Bunim.

Chasidic tradition tells us that everyone was concerned with the young man, who was gripped with sadness and absorbed in thought. His colleagues were uneasy about his strange, tattered garb and even stranger behavior. When he was advised to seek financial support from the wealthy patroness Tamaril, who was known for her great generosity, he reacted violently; when he heard the word money, he would jump to his feet as if bitten by a snake and spit.[17]

While in Peshischa, the adolescent Menachem Mendel began to exhibit his leadership qualities. Around him gathered a group of young men with sharp minds and scholarly reputation, possessed with an unyielding desire to live up to the high standards they had set for themselves.

It is reported by a contemporary that in the hall leading to Rabbi Simcha Bunim's study he found a young man pacing the floor energetically and engrossed in his thoughts, a tobacco box in his hand. The visitor, wanting to engage him in conversation, asked him for a sniff of tobacco. The young man did not even grace him with a glance. The visitor was soon surrounded by a gang of men, who grabbed him and threw him out from the hall. The next day he found the same strange young man standing with a huge volume of the Rif compendium in his hand, his right leg on a chair, and absorbed in silent study; the latter did not utter a word, but gesticulated constantly with his fingers. In this unusual position he remained from five o'clock in the morning, long before morning prayer time, until seven in the evening.[18]

This strange young man was Menachem Mendel. He was idolized by his friends, but opposed bitterly by others, who could not agree with his radicalism. They suspected him of aiming to become a tzaddik on his own. Once they asked him if he intended to be like the Besht. To their amazement they received a straightforward answer: "And so what? Did the Besht forbid us to compete with him or even to outshine him?"[19]

The small group of intimates that gathered around Menachem Mendel set up for itself the following goals: 1) To study the Talmud intensively; 2) Not to do anything without inquiring into the causes and effects of their deeds; and 3) Community-loving and faithfulness to the group. It was from these basic principles that Rabbi Menachem Mendel began to develop his own brand of chasiduth in Tomashov.

No matter how strongly Menachem Mendel was attached to "The Jew" or admired Rabbi Simcha Bunim, he could not restrain himself from seeking direction and guidance elsewhere, too. From time to time he left Peshischa and cruised around the different chasidic centers; he could be found with the Maggid of Kozenitz, Rabbi David of Lilow, and Rabbi Leibush of Shidlovtza. Years later he recalled: "I spent half-a-year with Rabbi Leibush of Shidlovtza and nobody knew me there. I was penniless and miserable, constantly exposed to the pangs of hunger and agony of colds. During an entire winter I slept in an attic exposed to the wind and rain. When I forgot myself in prayer and put my bleeding hands on the walls, they froze and stuck to the bricks. I was constantly in want and there was darkness all around me. I was on the brink of death."[20] But physical sufferings did not affect his spirit. He had an iron will and a steadfast determination to achieve perfection.

Menachem Mendel knew his own worth and strove consciously for leadership. Once, Rabbi Simcha Bunim came to a strange town with his retinue of disciples. The townspeople made a reception and honored him with wine. In turn, the rabbi invited different people to partake from this wine, but overlooked Menachem Mendel. After the strangers left, Menachem Mendel approached Rabbi Simcha Bunim and told him: "Of all your students I am the most outstanding. However, when it came to honors you forgot about me."[21] Only an aspirant to leadership could have behaved in such a way.

As Rabbi Simcha Bunim grew older, he became more and more dependent on Menachem Mendel, who "held his rabbi's hand and made all the arrangements for him."[22] When Rabbi Simcha Bunim lost his eyesight, Menachem Mendel came to his bedroom every night and read from the Zohar.[23] The moderates among the Peshischa chasidim were not too happy with the increasing power and influence of the "wild" Menachem Mendel. His tongue knew no restraint; nobody, no matter how important and high-placed, was immune from his pointed and sarcastic castigations. Nothing short of perfection pleased him; his anger was aroused by the stories about the "wonders and miracles" that the chasidic rebbes performed. "Wonders and miracles are executed in the land of the ignorant," he declared, paraphrasing a verse from the prayerbook (based on Psalms 105:27).[24] These utterances caused much opposition and ill will towards all the Peshischa chasidim and their teachings. Once, they were threatened with excommunication, supposedly issued against them by all the other Polish chasidic rabbis.[25]

"Rabbi Simcha Bunim's ways might have been acceptable to the people," many chasidic leaders were quoted to have said, "but the ways of his most important student were like thorns in their eyes and they could never agree to them."[26] To the chagrin of all these chasidic notables, this *enfant terrible* was destined to cause them much more embarrassment.

Chapter 5 — Notes

The Torah utterances of the Rabbi of Kotzk are scattered in some thirty collections of sayings and episodes of the lives of the chasidic greats. Almost every one of his pronouncements came down to us in a number of versions; it is nearly impossible to determine which of these are the authentic versions, because they were not put into writing immediately after they were said. Oral tradition transmitted the teachings of Rabbi Menachem Mendel from father to son, and from son to grandson; only the third generation committed them to writing. However, the fact that a number of authors repeated the same utterances, though in somewhat different form, should serve as a proof of their authenticity.

All the known sayings of Rabbi Menachem Mendel of Kotzk were collected by a group of "young chasidim" and put together in one volume, *Amud Ha'Emet*. Many of the quotations in this and in the following chapters are taken from this collection. However, at times it was necessary to reach to the original sources, because they are more colorful and explicit.

1. Some chasidic writers dispute this fact and make out of him a scion of an important rabbinic family. See P. Z. Gliksman, *Der Kotzker Rebbe*, p. 7; also Meyer Schwartzman, *Der Yiddisher Flam*, p. 352. Our account follows I. Arigur's *Kotzk*, p. 48; and E. Steinman's *Be'er HaChasidut*.
2. *Be'er HaChasidut*, p. 272

3. *Emet V'Emuna,* par. 786
4. *Emet V'Emuna,* par. 689
5. *Be'er HaChasidut,* p. 274
6. *Amud Ha'Emet,* p. 87
7. *Emet V'Emuna,* par. 261
8. *Emet V'Emuna,* par. 690
9. *Emet V'Emuna,* par. 790
10. *Sefer Abir HaRoim,* p. 44
11. Arigur, *Kotzk,* p. 51
12. Arigur, *Kotzk,* p. 53
13. *Amud Ha'Emet,* p. 98
14. *Be'er HaChasidut,* p. 273
15. *Amud Ha'Emet,* p. 101
16. *Amud Ha'Emet,* p. 301
17. *Siach Sarfey Kodesh,* par. 388
18. Marcus, *HaChasidut,* pp. 136-140
19. *Be'er HaChasidut,* p. 280
20. *Be'er HaChasidut,* p. 281
21. *Emet V'Emuna,* par. 325
22. *Emet V'Emuna,* par. 780
23. *Arzey HaLevanon,* p. 80
24. The same saying is also attributed to Rabbi Simcha Bunim.
25. See Chapter four, note 8
26. *Meir Eyney Hagola,* p. 185

Chapter 6

"In Tomashov a Fire
Is Burning Bright"

In 1827 Rabbi Simcha Bunim died, and a split appeared in the ranks of the orphaned chasidim. Some of them clung to the deceased leader's son Rabbi Abraham Moses, who was a considerate and popular individual, while others regarded Rabbi Menachem Mendel as the spiritual heir of Rabbi Simcha Bunim.

It has already been noted that, even during the lifetime of Rabbi Simcha Bunim, Menachem Mendel exerted considerable influence upon the extremist circles in his master's court. He attracted to himself many of the young men who possessed sharp minds and a profound knowledge of the Torah, and who were dissatisfied with the middle-of-the-road stand of their rabbi. These young zealots sought a more radical formulation of the Peshischa chasidic philosophy, and they became enthused with Menachem Mendel's incisive expressions and extremist ideas. They wanted him as their leader. The establishment of ruling dynasties of tzaddikim, which became accepted among the chasidim, was abhorrent to them. Not the son of the deceased but his most promising disciple should succeed him. In the "holy revolt" of Menachem Mendel they saw the fulfillment of their desires and placed all the passion of their youth at his disposal.

Menachem Mendel was not at his master's bedside at the time of the latter's death. Rabbi Simcha Bunim urged him not to delay his son's wedding on account of his illness. When Menachem Mendel returned to Peshischa it was already after the funeral; however, he showed no signs of remorse over missing his rabbi's funeral. He asked for the key to the deceased's room and locked himself up for a few hours. When he came out, he told the gathered chasidim that none of them was at the rabbi's funeral. Only he had been there.[1] He soon left Peshischa, explaining that he was not attached to the rabbi's body, only to his spirit.

As Menachem Mendel walked out, he left the bewildered chasidim with one more of his characteristic bolts. A village Jew came to Peshischa to ask Rabbi Simcha Bunim for Divine interference against the viciousness of his landlord. However, the rabbi was dead and there was no one to help him. As he stood in the hallway crying, he was advised to turn to Menachem Mendel for a blessing.

In reply, Menachem Mendel poured out a scornful lecture about the fools whose heads and hearts were empty of Torah and seemed to believe that a trip to a rebbe's court would substitute for the study of the Holy Torah and the worship of God.

"Had the Chosen People come down to the level of cattle?"[2] he cried. "The Torah was given at Sinai with roars of thunder and flashes of lightning. The masses of the people, however, seemed to be impressed with the externals of thunder and lightning but missed the deep meaning of the Torah." Later he said, "You may sway your body in prayer and still be removed from Torah."[3] Was all this an indication from Menachem Mendel to the startled chasidim, who gathered to elect a rabbi, that he would not be an amiable, tenderhearted leader but a man of principles? No matter what others would like him to do, he was not going to mellow just for the sake of winning their support.

The majority of the Peshischa chasidim, led by Rabbi Isaac of Vorka (deceased 1898), felt repelled by the high-mindedness exhibited by Menachem Mendel. They wanted a rabbi who would guide them, show compassion for their imperfections, and demonstrate interest in their welfare. They desired a rabbi with a heart, not a driving conscience. Their choice was the soft-spoken and compassionate Abraham Moses, the son of their deceased rabbi. The others, concerned with the novel Peshischa school of chasiduth that fused learning with the teachings of the Besht, declared Menachem Mendel their rabbi.

Chasidic tradition attributes to Isaac Meir, later the first rabbi of the Gerer chasidim (deceased 1866), the distinction of appointing Menachem Mendel to the post. The two, surrounded by their followers, met at a roadside inn and walked away into the forest, where they spent a whole night in conversation. In the morning they returned to the vigilant chasidim. Isaac Meir then took a measureful of water and poured it over the hands of Menachem Mendel; he later handed Menachem Mendel a towel to dry his hands. The puzzled disciples concluded that Isaac Meir had accepted the authority of Menachem Mendel. After breakfast the two locked themselves up again for an entire day. When the time for the evening prayers arrived, Isaac Meir emerged from the conference room and called on one of the chasidim to lead in the services because the rabbi would soon come to pray. Only then it became clear beyond doubt that Menachem Mendel would become rabbi.[4]

Rabbi Menachem Mendel was thirty-eight years old when he assumed leadership of the radical wing of the Peshischa chasidim in the year 1826. His residence was in Tomashov, in the district of Lublin, where he had lived since his marriage. Useless were all the efforts of the new Peshischa rabbi, Abraham Moses, to restore unity and attract Rabbi Menachem Mendel back to Peshischa. The man who was elevated to lead a group of chasidic enthusiasts did not believe in half-measures and compromises; "Only horses walk in the middle of the road," he used to say. His aim was originality, not unity. He was determined to bring about a renaissance of chasiduth and elevate it to unprecedented heights. He hoped for a chasidic movement that would attract the young Talmud scholars and convert them into men who lived on a higher intellectual and ethical plain. For himself he desired the status of a spiritual leader, who inspired his followers through his teachings and guided them in their own efforts to gain a deeper understanding of the Torah. He despised the chasidic rebbes who did nothing to dispel the ignorance of the masses and break down the walls of prejudice. He desired to bring the system of chasiduth, initiated by his predecessors in Peshischa, to its logical conclusion. In keeping with the Jewish tradition of learning, he was determined to bring his chasidim to the sources of the Jewish spirit, and utilize these values for personality enrichment and the leading of a truly Jewish way of life.

For this kind of a program Rabbi Menachem Mendel did not need many followers; he aspired to attract only a few, but of the highest intellectual and moral quality. "Ten righteous people would have saved Sodom, but a thousand fools could turn their leader into a fool," he was reported to have said to Rabbi Isaac of Vorka, who never tired of attempting to heal the break in the ranks of the former Peshischa chasidim.[5]

Rabbi Menachem Mendel's disciples expressed their contempt

75

for the kind of chasiduth conducted under the aegis of Rabbi Abraham Moses in Peshischa. "In Peshischa," they said, "there remains whiskey, a cart harnessed to four horses, the son of a tzaddik, and economic security." Meanwhile, Tomashov, under the guidance of Rabbi Menachem Mendel, was engaged in developing a kind of chasiduth that would be the crowning glory of all the manifold centuries of Jewish existence. Once he asked a disciple of his: "Tell me, for what purpose was man created?"

The disciple replied: "That he purify his soul."

"It is not so," said Rabbi Menachem Mendel. "It is man's duty to elevate the heavens."[6]

> "In Tomashov a fire is burning bright.
> From there shines the glow of a new light."[7]

This rhyme, together with the remarkable stories about the unusual rabbi who resided there, spread like wildfire throughout the different towns of Poland. Scores of young men, raised on the Talmud and captivated by the aura of chasidic legend, left their businesses and children in the hands of their wives and relatives, and trekked to Tomashov. Mindful of their rabbi's extremism, they divested themselves of all mundane responsibilities and gave all of themselves to the fulfillment of their rabbi's program. Rabbi Menachem Mendel scorned people who were only partially dedicated to his system. He used to say: "Only a true world is worthy of redemption, and if it cannot be true, let it not exist at all."[8]

Not everybody was afforded the honor of acceptance into the ranks of the Tomashov chasidim. People who were deficient in scholarship were told by Rabbi Menachem Mendel: "A Jew of your kind should not come to me; stay in your town and recite the

Psalms."⁹ When supplicants asked for a blessing, he retorted angrily that he was neither a magician nor a wizard; he himself suffered from want, and could not help himself. If all that did not scare away the petitioner and he still insisted that the rabbi pray for him, because the whole world knew that God listened to his prayers, then Rabbi Menachem Mendel would shout in anger: "The whole world says? Go, tell the whole world that they are fools and donkeys. Sustenance is in the hands of God. When the Jews came to Moses and Aaron in the wilderness and begged them for food, God replied to them: 'I will cause the heavens to rain bread for you' (Exodus 16:4). God Himself was the giver of bread, not Moses or Aaron, though they were fine and good Jews. If you are in need of bread, or you want children, go and pray to God yourself. God listens to everybody's prayers. You do not need an intermediary to carry your prayer to God."¹⁰

In Tomashov he gathered around himself about two hundred people who, according to the Talmudic saying, were capable of uprooting mountains in Jewish law. He fiercely hated the boor who aped and imitated, without attempting to develop his mind and powers of comprehension. In Rabbi Menachem Mendel's opinion, this mimic was dangerous, for just as a person accumulated everything easily, so was he prone to lose everything easily. Rabbi Menachem Mendel's dedication and persistent efforts towards the creation of a chasidic utopia attracted many of the future chasidic celebrities. Under his tutelage developed a large number of men who were destined to become leaders of the chasidic movement in the next generation.

Chanoch HaCohen (died 1870), the future Rabbi of Alexander, related how he became a disciple of Rabbi Menachem Mendel. "After the death of 'The Holy Jew,' I did not travel to any tzaddik, until finally I was attracted to Rabbi Bunim of Peshischa. Upon the latter's death, I again became desolate and I sat lost and confused, not knowing what new path to follow. And suddenly I fell into a deep sleep, and in my dream I found myself in Tomashov, and to my eyes was revealed a glorious vision of a flaming fire. I went then to Isaac Meir, the future rabbi of Ger, who interpreted my dream. He told me: 'Just as there were thunders and lightnings on Mount Sinai when the Torah was received, so is the Torah handed down with thunder and lightning in Tomashov today.' "[11]

The aforementioned Rabbi Isaac Meir, who by then was already referred to as the *iluy* (great young scholar) from Warsaw, once explained his lifelong devotion to Rabbi Menachem Mendel: "I perceived in him a living flame and I bent myself in adoration for thirty-two years. When I came to Tomashov and saw hundreds of young men devoting themselves to the study of chasiduth, I was sure that every one of them would grow up to become a Besht."[12] When rumors started to spread that Rabbi Isaac Meir had given up his allegiance to Rabbi Menachem Mendel, the latter became alarmed and wrote him a letter, which is worth quoting here:[13]

> I cannot restrain myself anymore and keep silent. I am worried because no letter from you reached me during the last three months. I feel lonesome even when I sit amidst beloved friends, and cannot find consolation among them. As I was in contact with you when I was in Warsaw, so I am now. Of all the people that were once in Peshischa, only the younger ones remained faithful to me; they are the ones who have courage in their hearts and look for light out of the darkness. All the others do not count. I am thinking only about you and I am looking for comfort from your letter.
>
> Four weeks ago, I sent a letter to you but no answer reached me. Please cheer me up with a letter. Also, because of the strife, I will not be able to sit here much longer, but this causes me much suffering and takes away my clarity of mind. I am worried about you and would not want to lose you. Because of my loneliness

I am not concerned too much with my adversaries. I must admit that many times we do not have enough to pay for the postage, otherwise I would write you more often. I remain your friend who wants the best for you.

This letter, written to a friend who was intellectually his equal, reveals the loneliness of a man who was surrounded by hundreds of enthusiastic admirers. Rabbi Menachem Mendel could teach and inspire his disciples, but he could not share his innermost thoughts with them. For this he needed a peer, and with the sole exception of Rabbi Isaac Meir there was nobody among the living to match him. This lack of suitable companionship may partly explain the crisis that overtook him later on.

Among the former followers of Rabbi Simcha Bunim of Peshischa there was one more man whose company he valued and with whom Rabbi Menachem Mendel liked to exchange ideas. This was Rabbi Isaac of Vorka. However, on almost all matters of chasidic theory and practice, they held diametrically opposing views. Chasidic tradition preserved a number of conversations between these two befriended opponents, conversations that throw much light on the personalities of the two distinguished parties.

A *mithnaged* once said to Rabbi Isaac: "The Talmud enumerates the many degrees of scholarship through which a man must advance before he attains the level of chasiduth (Abodah Zarah 20). Yet your men call themselves chasidim as soon as they visit a tzaddik." Rabbi Isaac defended the right of his men to call themselves chasidim, because they aspire to reach the standard of true chasiduth.

Rabbi Menachem Mendel, however, disagreed with him, and said: "A man should not style himself a chasid unless he is truly one. A few chosen persons may attain the degree of chasiduth without undergoing the preliminary steps. But when a multitude claim to do so, their pretensions are false, and it becomes imperative to return to the established manner of attaining chasiduth, through discipline and study.[14]

When the first *yahrzeit* of Rabbi Simcha Bunim was observed in Peshischa, to everybody's bewilderment Rabbi Menachem Mendel walked in. He then turned to Rabbi Isaac and explained his presence. "I did not come to the memorial; I am not a Jew who is attached to graves. I only came to see you."[15] When Rabbi Isaac mentioned to him his "unchasidic" behavior towards the simple people who came to seek his blessing and advice, Rabbi Menachem Mendel clarified his attitude by telling him the following story:

> There was once a billy goat, a holy goat whose great horns extended to the heavens. Every night, at midnight, the billy goat would straighten up and stand on his hind legs and extend his horns to the skies. When these horns touched the stars, the stars would commence singing. One day, a Jew from a village rose up early to go to the market and realized that he had lost his tobacco box. He began to search and search but with no results. The box had vanished and the Jew felt great sorrow upon the loss.
>
> The billy goat saw him sorrowing and out of sympathy extended his horns to him, for what wouldn't the holy billy goat do to ease the sorrow of a Jew? The Jew cut a piece of the goat's horn and carved out a tobacco box. He entered the house of study feeling happy, and out of generosity offered the Jews a pinch of his tobacco. The Jews had never smelled such a pleasant scent as that of this tobacco and they besieged the Jew with questions about his tobacco. He innocently replied that the tobacco was the same that he had always used but that the box was new. The Jews hurried to the marketplace and began to cut out pieces of the horns of the holy billy goat and carved tobacco boxes from the holy horns. The tobacco smelled fragrant, and the Jews enjoyed themselves, but the horns of the holy billy goat increasingly became smaller and did not reach the heavens any longer. And when midnight came, there was nobody to arouse the stars to song. . . . [16]

When, after two years of service as rabbi of the Peshischa chasidim, Rabbi Abraham Moses died, Rabbi Isaac of Vorka wanted to unite the two wings and came to Tomashov to offer Rabbi Menachem Mendel the leadership. However, Rabbi Isaac requested that he also treat the unscholarly chasidim in the same way his predecessors used to treat them.

Rabbi Menachem Mendel then replied: "In practicing seclusion I follow the way that the Torah indicated: 'When they bring me an offering take it from every man whose heart is willing' (Exodus 25:2). When a man seeks the truth, he should seclude himself from the men whose hearts are willing."

Rabbi Isaac disagreed with this interpretation and offered his own: "Join hands with every man whose heart is willing to bring an offering to God."[17] As had happened at previous occasions, the two disagreed and each followed his own ways, though they maintained friendly relations.

The two hundred people who joined Rabbi Menachem Mendel in Tomashov lived with him permanently without family or home. Young men abandoned their wives and refused to budge from the rabbi's court, turning a deaf ear to the bitter entreaties of wives and in-laws, who lamented the family ruin. There is substance to the story that even Rabbi Menachem Mendel paid no attention to the lamenting women and wailing children. The verse "Get out from your land and . . . from your father's house" (Genesis 12:1) he interpreted: "Get out from your earthly ways and from your habitual routine."[18]

"A chasid is a man who can throw away the entire world,"[19] and not be concerned with wife and family, but only with truth and redemption. "Messiah sits at the gates of Jerusalem and waits for an opportunity to throw off the shackles from his hands. Only truly devoted Jews, dedicated to God and the truth, will free him from his imprisonment and bring redemption."[20]

Earthly needs and material goods meant nothing in the feverish atmosphere of Tomashov. Here people were preoccupied with eternity and the eternal problems of the Jewish spirit. They were brought together in a fellowship of affection and dedication to the same interests. Whatever they had they shared joyfully. Their rabbi did not accept gifts from supplicants; he never knew where his next meal would come from, and cared even less. As he wrote in the letter to Rabbi Isaac Meir, a postage stamp presented at times a formidable obstacle. And so the chasidim who made Tomashov their residence had no choice but to work. Some of them were sent to work daily; the wages were spent on a collective meal with whiskey and bread to feed their souls. All were happy, for there was an inner joy which stemmed from each individual's personality and was warmed by the flaming fire that emanated from their rabbi.

For the chasidim these were memorable days. With delight they recalled the events of these years and retold them to their children and grandchildren. Once, at services on the Sabbath of Song (*Shabbat Shira*), the rabbi was called to the Torah. He recited the blessings with a strong and joyous voice. Then the reader read the assigned portion, and the rabbi repeated every word after him. When the verse "Then sang Moses and the children of Israel" (Exodus 15:1) was reached, the rabbi chanted together with the reader. His face beamed, his whole expression full of exaltation, and the entire synagogue was filled with joy. All present joined in chanting the Song of Redemption, as if they personally were redeemed from Egyptian bondage and crossed the Red Sea. The reader was transformed into a different person — every word of his was so distinctive that it penetrated deep into the heart. When he read "The Lord shall reign for ever and ever," even the walls of the synagogue trembled with jubilation. And later on, when Miriam took the cymbals and all the daughters of Israel sang and danced with her, everybody could feel the rabbi saying: Let rejoicing and cheerfulness come to all Israel.

After the Sabbath meal, all the chasidim gathered in the rabbi's house. The rabbi was in high spirits and began to sing the "Song of Redemption" and the chasidim sang with him. Then the chasidim formed a circle and started to dance; the rabbi joined them and danced with them for hours.[21]

Song and dance were frequent occurrences in Tomashov, and later in Kotzk. On Sabbath and festive days, when the chasidim became jubilant, old and young joined hands and danced together.[22] Many of the "Kotzker chants" became famous all over Poland and were remembered for many years. The musical taste of Rabbi Menachem Mendel was in consonance with his mental make-up. He disliked the outdrawn sad and sentimental tunes so common in chasidic music. He delighted in the joyous motifs of the march songs. And accordingly, the melodies used by his cantors were short, joyous, and expressive. The music had to interpret the prayers and not be regarded as an end in itself.[23]

One Sabbath night after the *kiddush,* his entire expression changed completely, and it seemed that he had divested himself of all corporeality. With all his strength he stretched out his hands for the ritual washing, and after the breaking of bread, he said: "There are many thinkers and philosophers who want to comprehend the Divine, but they cannot penetrate beyond the material limitations of their human intelligence. However, we, the children of Israel, are a holy nation; God gave us his commandments and through them we can perceive the Divine. This is the meaning of 'We will do and obey' (Exodus 24:7). When we will obey, we will reach ever-higher levels of perception of the Divine."[24]

Within Rabbi Menachem Mendel himself, two powerful forces battled — forces that he could not always reconcile. On the one hand, he was strongly attracted by the logical grandeur of the Talmud and of Maimonides' *Guide of the Perplexed*; on the other, he felt close to the mystical tradition of the Zohar and the teachings of the Ba'al Shem Tov. Consciously and conscientiously he strove to effect a synthesis between these two indigenous Jewish traditions.

However, he was too intelligent and self-critical to be satisfied with half measures and quasi-answers. He began with a strong propensity towards the rational, which he endeavored to attune and sensitize for the perception of the mystical. But in doing so, he was caught in a dilemma which defied solution. Into the essential democratic chasidic-religious movement, saturated with sympathy and love for the lower and uneducated, he injected an aristocratic element of intellectual distinctiveness and exclusiveness. He demanded of his chasidim that they develop the powers of self-analysis and introspection. He believed that every chasid could become a rabbi himself, if he developed all his latent, inner powers. Rabbi Menachem Mendel did not aim at mass-mindedness, but at critical discrimination. As he told Rabbi Isaac Meir: "A chasid is a man who ponders over every word and deed of his and inquires of himself: 'What do I want to achieve through them?' "[25]

A chasid should live not only on a high intellectual plane, but also on a high ethical plane. From his chasidim he demanded moral perfection and abrogation of all selfish considerations, which hinder communion with God. The chasidim developed prayer into an exceptional art, and many fabulous, awe-inspiring stories were told about the peculiar ways in which the chasidic celebrities prayed.

In this respect, too, Rabbi Menachem Mendel carried on the chasidic tradition he had inherited from his predecessors in Peshischa. The Polish chasidim, in fulfillment of the Scriptural verse: "All my bones will say, 'God who is like thee'" (Psalms 35: 1), used to pray aloud and even shout out entire sentences, gesticulating with their hands and swinging their bodies. On the contrary, the Peshischa way was to pray inwardly, without exhibiting any external motions. Rabbi Simcha Bunim used to say that when a Jew prayed his posture should remain erect, and only the soul should worship with thunder and lightning. Noting the verse "All my bones will say," he interpreted, "My entire inner being will say" (*atzmothay — atzmiyuth*), there will be no room in my soul for anything but God."

When Rabbi Menachem Mendel stood in prayer, he was uplifted in exaltation, but remained outwardly silent and motionless. Once, when "The Holy Jew" was on his deathbed and the synagogue filled with the cries and lamentations of the chasidim, Menachem Mendel stood quiet and soundless. Then Rabbi Simcha Bunim approached him, saying: "Menachem Mendel, why are you alarming all the heavens?"

He replied, "If this is God's will, there is no use to keep on imploring so stubbornly."[26]

Like all other Peshischa chasidim, Rabbi Menachem Mendel did not adhere to the time limitations set aside for prayer by the Shulchan Aruch. He took at face value the opinion of Rabbi Simeon, "Regard not thy prayer as a fixed mechanical task, but as an appeal for mercy and grace" (Aboth 2:18). He prayed only while in the proper frame of mind for prayer. Wild rumors spread about the Tomashover (and later Kotzker) chasidim. At midnight one might meet them scurrying for water for the afternoon prayer. To those who protested against this new custom, they replied that worship of the Creator was not to be regarded as a matter of daily routine, but as a contractual obligation.

All these new ways of Rabbi Menachem Mendel and his chasidim stirred up opposition, creating much strife. The adherents of the other chasidic rebbes could not forgive him the ridicule and ill-repute heaped on them and on their miracle-working rebbes. The opponents to chasidim, unable to understand his deviation from Jewish law for prayer, regarded him as a dangerous innovator. Strange stories circulated about him, and there were even eyewitnesses who claimed they had seen him smoking his pipe on the Sabbath.[27]

The most disappointed of all were the people of Tomashov. They expected that the establishment of a chasidic center in their midst would bring an economic boom to their city. Instead, they had to contend with hundreds of paupers and eccentrics. They were particularly irked by the cries of the suddenly "widowed" young wives who could not induce their husbands to come back home. To everybody around him in Tomashov, Rabbi Menachem Mendel seemed to be a puzzling, if not hated, personality. He could not endure this atmosphere for long, and after a stay of about two years in Tomashov, he accepted the invitation of the Rabbi of Kotzk, one of his followers, and moved to Kotzk.

Chapter 6 — Notes

1. *Meir Eyney Hagola,* par. 184
2. Arigur, *Kotzk,* p. 35
3. *Amud Ha'Emet,* p. 24
4. *Emet V'Emuna,* par. 791
5. Arigur, *l. c.,* p. 64
6. *Amud Ha'Emet,* p. 93
7. Unger, *Fun Peshischa bis Kotzk,* p. 125
8. Arigur, *l. c.,* p. 44
9. Schwartzman, *Der Yiddisher Flam,* p. 346
10. Schwartzman, *Der Yiddisher Flam,* p. 342
11. *Meir Eyney Hagola,* par. 194
12. *Emet V'Emuna,* par. 796
13. *Emet V'Emuna,* p. 137
14. Newman, *Hasidic Anthology,* p. 165, par. 9
15. *Amud Ha'Emet,* p. 119
16. Abraham Byk, *Yesod Ha'Omanut BaChasidut,* in *Hadoar,* Tamuz 5705
17. *Amud Ha'Emet,* p. 117
18. *Amud Ha'Emet,* p. 9
19. Schwartzman, *l. c.,* p. 360
20. Arigur, *l. c.,* p. 38
21. Bergman, *Kotzker Mayses,* pp. 143-146
22. Marcus, *HaChasidut,* p. 183
23. Geshuri, M. S., *Negina U'Menagnim b'Kotzk,* pp. 183-6, in *Heychal Kotzk* (edited by Rothenberg and Shenfeld)
24. *Emet V'Emuna,* par. 316
25. *Amud Ha'Emet,* p. 101
26. Schwartzman, *l. c.,* p. 360
27. Gliksman, *l. c.,* p. 45

Chapter 7

The Promise of Kotzk

In 1829, Rabbi Menachem Mendel moved to Kotzk and became famous as the Kotzker Rabbi. His system of chasiduth assumed the town's name. What took place in Tomashov was just a prologue to what would soon happen in Kotzk. Here the revolutionary system of chasiduth reached maturity and later broke down.

Kotzk was located to the east of Warsaw, on the highway leading to the Polish capital. It was much more accessible than Tomashov, which lay far to the south. Kotzk could even be reached on foot from many surrounding, densely populated Jewish townships. The fame of the Holy Man of Kotzk, so fundamentally different from all the other chasidic rabbis, spread like wildfire, and thousands of admirers and devotees from far and near trod the roads leading to Rabbi Menachem Mendel's new residence.

Just as on the roads to Jerusalem before the three great festivals, the roads to Kotzk were filled with pilgrims who trekked to their rabbi in fulfillment of the Scriptural commandment, "Three times in the year all thy males shall appear before the Lord God" (Exodus 23:17). In the minds and hearts of the chasidim, Kotzk took the place of Jerusalem, and these feelings were given expression in the song: "To Kotzk we do not ride, to Kotzk we walk on foot, Kotzk is in place of the Temple."[1] Crowds reached the magnitude of seven thousand — numbers that staggered the imagination in those times — leaving behind wives and children, and coming to Kotzk to celebrate the holidays in the shadow of Rabbi Menachem Mendel's presence. An air of festivity filled the streets. Jubilant crowds were always singing and dancing on the square before the rabbi's house.[2]

Only rarely did Rabbi Menachem Mendel, the object of all this admiration, join the festive crowds. And as time went on, these occasions became rarer still. As the number of his chasidim continued to grow, he became more contemplative and withdrawn. He was not interested in the size of his following, but in its quality.

At about the same time that Rabbi Menachem Mendel moved to Kotzk, Rabbi Abraham Moses of Peshischa died. Rabbi Isaac of Vorka grabbed at the chance to have all the former chasidim of Rabbi Simcha Bunim united under the aegis of Kotzk. Rabbi Menachem Mendel, however, was interested in "truth," and not in unity or peace. He was of the opinion that "any controversy which is motivated by the name of Heaven" (Aboth 5:20) and concerned with the search for truth is of enduring value. And where there is no "controversy motivated by the name of Heaven," there is no truth.[3]

In keeping with Hillel's adage, "An ignorant man cannot be a chasid" (Aboth 2:6), Rabbi Menachem Mendel often showed his displeasure with the multitudes that came to him. Once he complained before Rabbi Isaac Meir: "I do not know why they flock to me. During the six days of the week they do whatever pleases them, but when the Sabbath comes, they put on their festive garments and fur hats and regard themselves to be closely related to the Sabbath. I can tell you that on the Sabbath they are essentially the same as during the six weekdays."[4]

Rabbi Menachem Mendel craved for chasidim who were interested not only in themselves and their families, but with "elevating the heavens." During his first years in Kotzk, he was interested in attracting Talmudic scholars to whom scholarship alone was not enough. He wanted chasidim who searched for a life of meaning and fulfillment through the practice of Jewish ethics and by delving into the innermost layers of the Jewish scholarly tradition. The former students of the Talmudic academies who after marriage left wife and kin to stay with him in Kotzk were especially to his liking. Many of these were the students of Rabbi Isaac Meir, whose influence drew them to "the holy flame" that flickered in Kotzk.

Rabbi Menachem Mendel, however, lacked the patience to deal personally with these promising young men. He usually left them under the tutelage of his trusted disciple Mordecai Joseph Leiner, the future rabbi of Izbitza. Only from time to time would he himself walk into the precincts of the *beth hamidrash* (study house). He would glance into the open volumes and into the faces of the students, engage somebody in a pungent exchange of opinions, utter a few pointed remarks, and then disappear. These utterances of his were later the subject of conversation; chasidim used to ponder and deliberate over them for years, until they understood what their sainted rabbi meant by them.

Rabbi Abraham Borenstein (died 1910), author of books on Talmudic law, a son-in-law of Rabbi Menachem Mendel, and later the rabbi of Sochatzev, once said that only forty years after the event did he understand a saying of his father-in-law.

Once, Rabbi Abraham took sick and there was little hope for his recovery. During his sickness, Rabbi Menachem Mendel never came to visit him. When Rabbi Abraham's father inquired as to the strange treatment accorded his son and mentioned that his son used to spend twenty hours a day in study, Rabbi Menachem Mendel replied: "And this you consider study?" A few days later, Rabbi Abraham recovered, but his father could neither understand nor forget Rabbi Menachem Mendel's remark.

Forty years later, Rabbi Abraham gained comprehension of this remark while studying the Jerusalem Talmud with his students. According to the Zohar, every man enters this world for the sake of fulfilling some duty he had neglected in a previous metempsychosis; he does not die until he has completed the mission assigned him. Observation of an individual is enough to reveal which of the 613 commandments it is his duty to fulfill. The Jerusalem Talmud tells of Rabbi Tarphon's serious illness. When his colleagues prayed to God and mentioned how meticulously he kept the commandment "Honor thy mother," his mother interrupted and said, "He did not even fulfill half of his duties towards his mother" (Kiddushin 1:7). Just as the prayers for Rabbi Tarphon should not have stressed his devotion to his mother, so should there have been no mention of Rabbi Abraham's devotion to study, for neither of them could die until he had fulfilled his obligation.[5]

Kotzk, preoccupied with matters of the spirit, had little time, and even less patience, for material things. It is true that Rabbi Menachem Mendel did not negate this world, at least not at the beginning of his career. But this did not prevent him from setting very high standards for the close circle of his disciples. They were solely absorbed in study and moral perfection. Their earthly needs were satisfied with a bit of whiskey and dry bread, which they purchased by selling their wedding presents. At times Tamaril, the wealthy chasidic matron, came to their aid and freely distributed funds to the trusted chasidim, despite the rabbi's objections. The enthusiasm of the Kotzker chasidim was unlimited, their consecration and abnegation complete. If in Tomashov there were chasidim who might have worried about their poverty, in Kotzk there was not even the memory of such sentiments. There was no concern for wife, children, or livelihood. The flaming chasidic spirit swept away everything before it, and was kept alive by the presence of the rabbi and his teachings.

The only occupation of the chasidim in Kotzk was study. First of all, a chasid in Kotzk had to be learned if he aspired to be accepted and noticed. In the beginning, the rabbi himself supervised the study of the more promising disciples; as he gradually withdrew more and more into himself, Mordecai Joseph Leiner guided the studies in his stead.[6] Upon their rabbi's insistence, the most common subject of study was the Babylonian Talmud; only those already conversant in it were encouraged to read Maimonides' philosophical work and the Zohar. Whenever Rabbi Menachem Mendel noticed a chasid whom he regarded as an insufficient authority in Talmud reading the *Guide of the Perplexed,* he would whisper into the man's ear that to the one who had his fill of Talmud, Maimonides was a guide — but to the one who lacked a sound knowledge of Talmud, he was perplexing.[7]

It was the aim of Rabbi Menachem Mendel to effect a symbiosis between the rational philosophy of Maimonides and the mystical teachings of the Zohar. As time went on, he attached more and more importance to understanding and motivation than to the actual performance of the commandments. "Saintliness is achieved through deeds, but some others achieve saintliness through their brains."[8] He poked fun at the so-called "pious" who "make out of the incidental the most essential, and out of the most essential — an incidental." The difference between a chasid and a *mithnaged* he defined to mean that "A chasid has reverence for God, and a *mithnaged* for the laws of the Shulchan Aruch." On another occasion he formulated the same idea in different words. He said: "There is a prohibition against making idols out of the Divine commandments. We should never imagine that the chief purpose of a commandment is its outward form, to which the inward meaning should be subordinated. The very opposite is the position we should take."

Rumors began to circulate among the Jews of Poland and Galicia. The chasidic rabbis and their followers were alarmed by the supposedly chasidic rabbi of Kotzk who was upsetting the whole chasidic way of life. Aaron Marcus, a contemporary writer, himself favorably disposed towards chasiduth and the first to present the chasidic movement in terms acceptable to West European Jews, saw in Rabbi Menachem Mendel a menace to the system established by Rabbi Israel Ba'al Shem Tov.

> The older chasidim raised an outcry against the teachings of Rabbi Menachem Mendel and pointed out how dangerous they were, without knowing how to explain their objections properly, save for some minor details. The former Talmudic scholars turned chasidim have forgotten that they used to mock the chasidim for their belief in the tzaddikim, and now they themselves worship Rabbi Menachem Mendel to such an extent that they will not call him by his name, but by the designation "Let him live for many years."

The most outspoken of his chasidic opponents was Rabbi Israel of Rizhin (died 1850), who announced that the Rabbi of Kotzk was his opposing pole.[10] Rizhin and Kotzk clashed on the entire front and advocated diametrically opposite opinions on Torah, prayer, conduct, manners, dress, beliefs and opinions, family origins, and — most of all — the relationship between the tzaddik and his chasidim.

The *mithnagdim* could not understand the lighthearted manner in Kotzk toward prayer as set by the Shulchan Aruch. Now they had more reasons for worry. Snap remarks of Rabbi Menachem Mendel and his supposed disregard for many hallowed distinctive marks of Jewish piety were beyond their power of comprehension. The whole system of Jewish life in the Diaspora was built upon the foundation of observance of the manifold commandments, which formed the distinctively Jewish way of life. Understanding and motivation were only of secondary importance, and could in no way interfere with the established canons of Jewish behavior.

However, said the *mithnagdim*, the Rabbi of Kotzk, who commanded so much adoration from so many scholarly Jews, seemed to be unconcerned with all this. So singlemindedly absorbed was he with his self-imposed task of developing a new system of chasiduth that he did not notice that in doing so he was destroying the very foundation of Jewish life. Was Rabbi Elijah of Wilno right when he suspected that the "sect" would bring dissension, and maybe even a schism, into Jewish life?

Only the atmosphere of fear, suspicion, and misunderstanding that surrounded all the doings of the Kotzker Rabbi could explain the strange treatment meted out to him by many religious leaders and literary figures. A movement was on the way in Poland to excommunicate Rabbi Menachem Mendel and all his chasidim; only the strong stand taken by Rabbi Akiba Eiger of Posen saved the day for Kotzk. The rabbi of Lvov, who for awhile believed the rumors that Rabbi Menachem Mendel smoked a pipe on the Sabbath while visiting a physician in Lvov, was ready to take action against him.[11]

The only ones who could be happy with these strange stories about "the rabbi turned unbeliever" were the *maskilim,* the small group of modernists who wanted to bring "enlightenment" to the Jew and "westernize" him.

In the face of all these strange accusations and false reports, Rabbi Menachem Mendel was unmoved. He remained steadfast and firm in his conviction that his chosen road was the right one. Elaborating on the Scriptural verse: "And we were in our own sight as grasshoppers and so we were in their sight" (Numbers 13:33), he explained, "The scouts that Moses sent from the wilderness to explore the Promised Land looked like grasshoppers when compared to the local giants — this I can understand. But why did they have to say, 'and so we were in their sight'? What does it matter to you how you look in the eyes of others?"

Maimonides commented on the words "Let us make man" (Genesis 1:26) that God was not concerned at all with the fools who might conclude that there were many deities because the Bible used the plural form "us."[12] The Rabbi of Kotzk remained unconcerned with the opinions of others about himself and his system. He sought neither approval nor disapproval, but the truth; and the truth did not depend on majority consent. "No majority in the entire world can decide what is truth." "The Holy Jew" taught his disciples that "the one who mocks himself can also mock the entire world."[13] And in this regard, too, Rabbi Menachem Mendel drew the final, logical conclusions from the teachings he had gleaned from his Peshischa predecessors.

It would be erroneous to present his aims as the understanding and the refining of judgment for their own sake. For the Rabbi of Kotzk desired from his students thought and critical evaluation "for the sake of Heaven." Let us not forget even for a moment that Rabbi Menachem Mendel was as much a mystic as a rationalist; if he advocated rational discrimination in the worship of God, he also insisted on communion with God and on a mystical apprehension of the irrational in the Torah and the Divine. "A God whom I could understand, I would not have chosen," he was quoted as having said a number of times.[14]

Highly characteristic of Rabbi Menachem Mendel's attitude is the following story told about him:

> Once a chasid came to him, complaining: "Rabbi, I am forced to think and think constantly and I cannot find peace of mind."
> "About what are you thinking so much?" inquired Rabbi Menachem Mendel.
> "I am wondering if there is a Supreme Judge, who deals with the world justly," relied the chasid.
> "What does it matter to you?" asked the rabbi.
> "Rabbi, if there is no Judge and no justice, then all of creation does not make sense."
> "And what does it matter to you?" asked the rabbi.
> "Rabbi, if there is no Judge and no justice, then what sense does the entire Torah make?"
> "And why does it matter to you?" insisted the rabbi.
> "How can you say that, Rabbi? Surely it matters to me!"
> "If you are so concerned, then you must be a good Jew. A good Jew is allowed to think; it will do you no harm," consoled Rabbi Menachem Mendel.[15]

This beautiful chasidic tale so expressively touches upon the core of Rabbi Menachem Mendel's personality and world outlook. Man, endowed by his Creator with reason, is duty-bound to examine everything critically; however, there are limitations to the rule of reason. God is beyond the grasp of reason and His essence cannot be comprehended logically. God is apprehended intuitively. It is man's duty to comprehend and apprehend simultaneously.

How could this be achieved? In what way did Rabbi Menachem Mendel hope to achieve this desired symbiosis between the teachings of Maimonides and the exhortations of the Zohar? One saying of his, picked from many similar to it, might serve as a good introduction to this subject.

"The man who studies Torah but not exhaustively, sins and forgives himself, prays only because he prayed yesterday — a complete evil-doer is better than he."[16] Study, the practice of ethics, and prayer were the three paths by which the Rabbi of Kotzk hoped to achieve the desired comprehension and apprehension of the Divine.

Much has already been said about the importance attached to learning by the Rabbi of Kotzk; more will be said about it in an ensuing chapter. However, learning was only the beginning in the scheme of Kotzk. The verse "Wherefore is the land perished?. . . Because they have forsaken My Torah" (Jerermiah 9:11-12) — he expounded to mean: "They (the *mithnagdim*) did not study the Torah for the purpose of carrying out its teachings in life. Study remained with them the beginning and the end, and therefore did the land perish."[17] Not so with Rabbi Menachem Mendel of Kotzk, who aimed with his teaching to reach "the umbilicus of the listener" and transform him into a different human being.

When, in his youth, the grandfather of the author of *Der Yiddisher Flam* came to Kotzk before Rosh Hashana, he was asked by David, the oldest son of Rabbi Menachem Mendel: "Young man, did you already clear the leaven?" The chasid stood bewildered, not understanding what the clearing of the leaven had to do with Rosh Hashana. David came forth with an explanation:

"Young man, you should know that just as it is the duty of a Jew to clear the material leaven before Passover, so are we obliged to remove the leaven from the soul before Rosh Hashana. Jealousy, covetousness, and glory are poisonous to the soul; labor constantly to better yourself — otherwise your coming here is in vain. There is no room here for do-nothings and incompetents."[18]

The faithful chasidim remained in Kotzk for months and even years, completely disinterested in things material. They did not know where their next meal would come from; whenever they received money or a package of victuals from home, they shared it readily with the others. Did their rabbi not teach them the rabbinic saying: "The Torah was given for interpretation to no one but to those who ate manna" (Mechilta, Beshalach)? This meant that only Jews who had not more than one day's living and cared little about the next day were in a position to study and understand the Torah properly.[19]

Their aim was not only to understand the Torah properly, but to carry out its moral precepts. They labored hard to tear out from themselves every tinge of selfishness, pride, and dependence on the judgments of others. They spent nights in study — not in the *beth hamidrash,* where they could be seen by others, but in the retreats of their lodging places, where nobody could watch them. They performed deeds inconspicuously and anonymously, so that nobody would find out about them. Their aspiration was to "walk humbly" (Micah 6:8), not only before God, but also with themselves — not to take pride in their doings even in the innermost thoughts of their hearts. An aphorism was formed: "Kotzker chasidim do transgressions in the open and good deeds in hiding." It was easier to catch a good Jew sinning than a Kotzker chasid performing a noble deed.[20]

After his son David recovered from a dangerous illness, Rabbi Menachem Mendel asked him what temptation had been the most difficult to overcome when he thought his last minute had arrived. To this David replied that he thought how nice it would be to shout out loud: "Hear, O Israel, the Lord, our God, the Lord is One" (Deuteronomy 6:4). However, he did not do so, and uttered his last prayer silently, so that nobody might hear him. Rabbi Menachem Mendel then put his hand on his son's shoulder and told him in an exalted voice: "David, you are a Kotzker chasid."[21]

Next to truth, Kotzk valued humility. The Kotzker Rabbi taught: Do not take pride in the fact that you are humble; "Be humble in your humbleness." Only when a man overcomes all. traces of selfishness and pride and becomes humble can he achieve saintliness and communion with God. The verse: "dwell in the land and cherish faithfulness" (Psalms 37:3), he interpreted: "Only when you sleep on the bare ground can you grow in belief." First you must give all of yourself to God. "And Abel, he also brought" (Genesis 4:4) was interpreted to mean that Abel brought all of himself to God; he completely renounced all of himself before God, and therefore God accepted his offering.[22]

The following song attributed to the Kotzker chasidim is characteristic of their attitude:

Where does God reside?
In whatever site He is invited.
Where is He allowed in?
Into a dwelling that's pure for Him.
What dwelling is pure for Him?
A man who walks humbly in His sight.[23]

Kotzk demanded from its adherents total dedication and complete consecration to the Divine. It knew of no compromise and no half-measures. The total person with all of his cognitive and intuitive powers was to be attuned to the understanding of God. "Man was created to elevate the heavens." "And [Jacob] lay down in that place" (Genesis 28:11) — he gave all of himself to that "place," and therefore he was privileged to commune with God.

All socially accepted conventions like learning, wealth, good manners, and family lineage meant absolutely nothing in Kotzk. Only what a man made of himself, to what use he put the things the Creator endowed him with — only this mattered to the Kotzker chasidim. They ridiculed learning that did not produce character and inner religiosity. The mere memorization of facts and the mechanical performance of the commandments were repugnant to them. They sought to rejuvenate religion through a synthesis of learning and religiosity — which could be achieved only through hard labor and continuous purposeful dedication. "I labored and found — believe him" (Megillah 6). "If you labored on the Torah, you found faith; however, if you did not labor on the Torah and you found — do not believe." Rabbi Menachem Mendel did not believe that people can walk on the path of righteousness without laboring on the Torah and without inner exertion. Some people are brought accidentally to the path of righteousness through stubbornness. Scripture refers to them when it cautions: "And that you go not about after your own heart and your own eyes" (Numbers 15:39).[24]

To the people who achieved this inner fusion of learning and faith, social respectability and accepted convention meant very little. The Rabbi of Kotzk and his faithful walked around in slippers and tattered rags; many chasidim covered their heads with cabbage leaves instead of a hat. Once, on the eve of Yom

Kippur, a Kotzker chasid saw a respectable Jew walking in his white overgarment (*kitel*) to the synagogue. The chasid asked him to borrow the white overgarment and rolled himself in the slush. Then he took it off and returned it to the bewildered owner.[25]

A good accounting of the Bohemianism and disregard for convention that pervaded human relationships in Kotzk is provided in the following story. Leib Eiger, later the tzaddik of Lublin (died 1838) and grandson of the famous Rabbi Akiba Eiger, came for the first time to Kotzk, wearing his most expensive garments. As he entered the house of study, his fur hat was knocked down, and the package under his arm was pulled out and sent to be pawned for cake and whiskey. Leib Eiger went to the rabbi and complained about the rough treatment accorded him. Rabbi Menachem Mendel ordered that everything taken from him be returned, commenting that this young man was not the proper material to become a Kotzker chasid.[26]

Nothing was more disdainful to Kotzk than self-assurance and pride in possessions unearned. Kotzk valued humbleness. When a visitor came and announced that he was a grandson of "The Holy Jew," Rabbi Menachem Mendel snapped back: "What a celebrity; you may go." Only after the visitor sat for a time in the hall, broken and despondent, was he suddenly called back. Rabbi Menachem Mendel then spent a long time with him, inquiring about his life and explaining the Kotzker system.

No opportunity to teach modesty was overlooked by the Kotzker Rabbi. Once, upon his recommendation, one of his chasidim was invited to serve as rabbi of the city of Biala. Overjoyed with the good news, the chasid came to Rabbi Menachem Mendel to thank him for his efforts on the chasid's behalf. Suddenly the Kotzker began to shout at him: "You have become a rabbi? How dare you accept such a position? Are you fit for it?" The newly appointed rabbi left the room dazed and heartbroken. Soon, however, he was called in and congratulated on his election.[27]

Once, a brother of this rabbi came to Kotzk to receive Rabbi Menachem Mendel's blessing. When, during the procedure of writing out his wish, he mentioned that he was the rabbi's brother, Rabbi Menachem Mendel told him angrily: "How can I know you, when I am not related even to myself?"[28] The mere idea that something could be attained without toil was abhorrent to the Kotzker mentality. Kotzk voiced loudly its protest against "the grandchildren" who inherited the mantles of chasidic leadership from their predecessors, through no virtue of their own. Kotzk opposed the foundation of "dynasties" of tzaddikim, and the existence of "rabbis" to whom dignity was considered a birthright. Kotzk recognized neither birthright nor inherited privilege. The idea of Kotzk was Abraham, the "self-made" man. Abraham the Patriarch, the son of a pagan, came through his own efforts and dedication to the truth, to a recognition of God. To a certain degree, every Jew is in Abraham's situation; everyone must, through his own efforts and by his own means, find the road leading to God.

To the Kotzker way of thinking, knowledge of God and communion with Him are not acts of grace and grants of undeserved privilege bestowed upon the chosen few, but accomplishments that can be achieved by anybody who honestly and wholeheartedly desires them. "But from there you will seek the Lord, your God; and you shall find Him, if you search after Him with all your heart and with all your soul" (Deuteronomy 4:29). If you search "from there," from the innermost spot of your heart, "you shall find" what you are after, and you will desire constantly, with all your heart and all your might, to know Him better and better.[29]

What is the role of the tzaddik, of the chasidic rebbe, in this constellation of total commitment to God? Rabbi Menachem Mendel envisaged himself as an educator — a spiritual leader, whose duty it was "to awaken the hearts of Israel to come close to God and learn His ways." Once he was told about another rebbe, who was rumored to have the power to work miracles. "I would like to know if he is able to perform the miracle of making one real chasid," was the reply of Rabbi Menachem Mendel.[30]

The education of the chasid was Rabbi Menachem Mendel's main function in life, and to this ideal he devoted himself wholeheartedly. He did not aspire to write books; all he needed was a living example — an incarnation of all the great ideas expounded in the books. He desired men of flesh and blood who would give substance and vitality to these ideas.

> Many times in the Torah man learns the laws and the commandments and the proper behavior, and after all that, he does not understand or know how to carry them out in life. When it comes to charity, humility, prayer, and other related commandments, man does not know how to fulfill them in the manner demanded by chasiduth. However, when he sees how a rebbe or a chasid fulfills these obligations, when he sees his enthusiasm, devotion, and refinement in the manner of carrying out the commandments, then he recalls what he had learned in the Torah and attempts to follow his rebbe in achieving perfection in the mode of performing the Divine teachings.[31]

This lengthy statement, ascribed to the Kotzker Rabbi by a grandson of one of his devoted chasidim, describes accurately his point of view.

Before this chapter can be brought to a conclusion, one more point of importance needs clarification. Did the Kotzker Rabbi perform all the customary chores of a chasidic tzaddik? Did he accept petitioners and advise them on their family and business problems? Did he bestow blessings and dispense prayers for the well-being of the sick and needy?

The available source material allows us to answer the questions, except the last, with a qualified "yes." Rabbi Menachem Mendel usually referred to himself with the appellation *a guter yid* (a good Jew), a term used in Yiddish for the designation of a chasidic leader. However, he was *a guter yid* of a different kind. Instead of the customary "signs and miracles," he tried to appear in the eyes of his disciples and petitioners as a man of wisdom and learning. The daily contact with the chasidim provided him with splendid opportunities to act as guide and teacher — a role he desired for himself.

The Kotzker Rabbi did not expect every one of his chasidim to be an accomplished scholar and a man preoccupied constantly with "elevating the heavens." A story is told about a Talmudic scholar who became so involved in his business that he was forced to forgo his studies. On a holiday visit to Kotzk, he bitterly complained about this. Rabbi Menachem Mendel consoled him and at the same time taught him a lesson in ethics: "At the conclusion of each chapter of the *Ethics of the Fathers,* we recite the passage of Rabbi Chananiah ben Akashia: 'The Holy One wished to benefit Israel; therefore, He gave them a multitude of commandments.' We may ask: Why is it a benefit to be duty-bound to observe so many commandments? This is a great hardship. Would it not be preferable to receive merely a limited number of precepts which we could fulfill properly? The answer is that the great variety of precepts makes it possible for a Jew in every occupation to obey some of the Divine injunctions. The farmer, the planter, the builder of houses, and others — each has his particular commandment to fulfill and thereby gain favor in the eyes of the Lord. The merchant also, by abstaining from misrepresentations, overcharges, and other business deceptions, will please the Creator."[32]

The Rabbi of Kotzk knew that not everybody can be wholly preoccupied with spiritual matters. "I could have made chasidim out of the whole world, but it would not be good." Men who are busy making a living should not be condemned, because this is the way the world has been structured.

"When you eat the labor of your hands, happy you shall be" (Psalms 128:2). This verse he interpreted to mean that "only your hands should be busy doing work and not your heart or brain. Man should dedicate his heart and brain to the service of God and not profane them with earthly matters."[33]

Work is a necessary evil, and man must learn to do all the things necessary to earn a living and nevertheless keep his mind above them. Even the busiest man should set aside at least one hour a day for the study of Torah.[34]

He gave advice to his chasidim on the conduct of their businesses. A number of such advices have been preserved by the descendants of his chasidim. Pinchas Zelig Gliksman, the author of a monograph on the Kotzker Rabbi, tells that his grandfather used to consult the rabbi on every important business matter. He had a partner with whom he did not get along too well and he often wanted to dissolve this partnership; but the rabbi did not agree to it. Once the rabbi asked him: "Did it ever happen that your partner had an opinion different from yours, and subsequent events proved him right?" When he received an affirmative answer, he said: "If so, what do you want?"[35]

When a chasid asked him how he could give advice on business affairs when he was so completely removed from all worldly preoccupations, the chasid received the following reply: "Sometimes an outsider sees more clearly than the one inside."

The following story is characteristic of the system of thought of Rabbi Menachem Mendel.

Once a chasid asked his advice about a marriage and received an evasive answer, with which he remained dissatisfied.

Then the Kotzker explained: "Do you really believe that when somebody comes to ask for my advice I go to heaven and open the book and look up what is inscribed there? It would be brazen insolence to maintain such an idea. What else happens? When somebody comes to ask me for advice, he makes me self-conscious. When somebody is preoccupied with his own importance, he loses his mental balance. So, first I must do away with my arrogance and regain cool judgment; and then I must consider if what I am going to say is in accord with the law of the Torah, and later on — if it is fair and just. Only after I have done all that can I give advice that is worthwhile."[36]

The affairs of life can be solved properly only when man arrives at a synthesis of humility and critical judgment, guided by the law of the Torah and considerations of fairness and justice.

Chapter 7 — Notes

1. Ehrlich, Israel, *Rabbi Mendele Mi'Kotzk,* p. 124.
2. Marcus, *HaChasidut,* p. 183
3. Gliksman, Abraham Hirsch, *Der Kotzker Rebbe,* p. 26
4. *Amud Ha'Emet,* p. 72
5. Schwartzman, *Der Yiddisher Flam,* pp. 369-371
6. Weisbrod, David, *Arzey HaLevanon,* p. 75
7. Schwartzman, *l. c.,* p. 349
8. Steinman, *Be'er HaChasidut,* p. 322
9. *Emet V'Emuna,* par. 770, 645; Newman, *The Hasidic Anthology,* p. 192
10. Marcus, *l. c.,* p. 183 and p. 18; see also Steinman, *l. c.,* p. 382

11. Gliksman, *l. c.,* p. 44-46; Alfasi, *Rabbi Menachem Mendel Mi'Kotzk,* pp. 43-44
12. Schwartzman, *l. c.,* p. 342, p. 347
13. *Amud Ha'Emet,* p. 5, Gliksman, *l. c.,* p. 27
14. Arigur, *Kotzk,* p. 137
15. Ehrlich, *l. c.,* p. 55
16. Buber, *Or HaGanuz,* p. 558
17. *Amud Ha'Emet, l. c.,* p. 52
18. Schwartzman, *l. c.,* p. 375
19. *Amud Ha'Emet, l. c.,* p. 95
20. Gliksman, *l. c.,* p. 33
21. Schwartzman, *l. c.,* p. 392
22. *Amud Ha'Emet, l. c., p. 6*
23. *Finkelstein, Megillat Polin,* p. 162
24. *Amud Ha'Emet, l. c.,* p. 33, p. 49
25. Marcus, *l. c.,* p. 183
26. *Emet V'Emuna,* par. 624
27. *Emet V'Emuna,* par. 141, *Amud Ha'Emet,* p. 127
28. Schwartzman, *l. c.,* p. 351
29. *Amud Ha'Emet,* p. 44
30. *Amud Ha'Emet,* p. 31, Newman, *l. c.,* pp. 260, 262
31. *Ohel Torah,* p. 109
32. Newman, *l. c.,* p. 77, par. 3
33. *Emet V'Emuna,* par. 105, 191
34. *Emet V'Emuna,* par. 163, 127
35. *Tiferet Adam,* p. 17
36. Newman, *l. c.,* p. 514, par. 3; Gliksman, *l. c.,* pp. 30-31

Chapter 8

The Crisis

It is not easy to point out when the first symptoms of the
coming crisis started to become evident. However, as time went
on, Rabbi Menachem Mendel's behavior and entire way of life
became so strange that even many of his most devoted disciples
failed to understand him. At the very time when he reached his
peak and the numbers of his followers were increasing, something
changed. The faithful chasidim, who flocked to Kotzk to bask in
their rabbi's glory and purify themselves in the soul-healing
atmosphere of his presence, felt that their rabbi was not his usual
self.

Throughout the day he was submerged in thought. His facial
expression indicated no pain, but rather sorrow and melancholy.
What was the explanation for this melancholy? Who had cast
upon Rabbi Menachem Mendel this spell of darkness? No one
knew the answer.

Neither Rabbi Menachem Mendel nor his closest chasidim left
records from which we might find the causes for the unusual
moods into which the founder of the Kotzk system had lapsed. All
we can do is examine the comments he occasionally uttered when
seized by melancholy, anguish, or weariness of soul.

Was Rabbi Menachem Mendel justified in accusing his

chasidim of forgery, deceit, and cheating? Was this a confession of lack of strength, or a subconscious recognition that the task of "raising the heavens" was beyond his reach? These thoughts enter the mind when we read about the excessive insults and abuse he heaped upon the heads of his disciples. Naturally, there were among his chasidim people who harbored material interests. Rabbi Menachem Mendel, endowed with a penetrating eye and a discerning heart, should have known that among his chasidim there were men who stood head and shoulders above the masses — men of sharp minds and spirited souls who were prepared to sacrifice everything in order to carry out the lofty ideals which he taught them. Could it be that Rabbi Menachem Mendel at times was unable to differentiate between the straight and the crooked? Would it be right to assume that this man of solid logic was confused and illogical? These are questions which must be solved by everyone who attempts to make intelligible the Kotzk story.

Because of the lack of more reliable indicators, we must look for the causes of Rabbi Menachem Mendel's change in his personality makeup and system of thought. As has already been pointed out, this man, endowed with such rare qualities of mind, was also subject to fits of temper and changing moods. The rational and irrational components of his personality did not always strike a happy balance. His exaltation was ennobling and radiating — and for this he was admired by his chasidim; but his sadness was gnawing, consuming, and depressing. His powers of mind and drives of emotion were beyond the range and reach of the ordinary.

Chasidic tradition relates that once a Russian general lost his jewel-studded tobacco box. He suspected that it was picked up by one of the chasidim who trekked to Kotzk on that road. Because chasidim were known to reveal all their secrets to their rebbe, the general intended to come to Kotzk, put the rebbe under oath, and request his cooperation in locating the treasure. As the general entered Rabbi Menachem Mendel's study, he was overcome by an irrational awe. He entreated the rabbi to tell him what power he had used in order to attract so many adherents. Rabbi Menachem Mendel explained that he could think about a problem for twenty-four consecutive hours, without having another thought enter his mind. To this the general replied that the rabbi must really be a divine man, because he himself could not concentrate on one thought even for a minute; usually a thousand thoughts occupied his mind simultaneously.[1]

This rare ability to concentrate and see through all the ramifications of a problem is evident in the hundreds of the Kotzker's aphorisms. Almost all his sayings are concise, pointed, and purposeful. His radicalism, his tendency to draw the final, most extreme conclusions from each idea with which he was preoccupied, was a direct outcome of his unusually high intelligence.

These exceptional powers of mind were applied by Rabbi Menachem Mendel to the study of Torah. Torah was his lifelong occupation and in its study he achieved an unusual degree of mastery. Among his close disciples were the greatest Talmudic scholars of his generation, and all of them had the greatest respect for the depth of his learning. Rabbi Isaac Meir, "the genius from Warsaw," accepted his opinion with humility and admiration even when it went contrary to his own previously expressed judgment. To him the Kotzker was "a *tanna* from Gemara."[2] The Kotzker's son-in-law, Rabbi Abraham of Sochatzev, reputedly one of the most profound Talmudists, never tired of saying that he

110

owed his understanding of the texts to his father-in-law.

The same Rabbi Abraham of Sochatzev recalled an incident involving himself and Rabbi Isaac Meir. It was then the accepted opinion among all Polish Talmudists that there was a certain error in the Mishna, which Rabbi Isaac Meir wanted to correct in an ensuing publication. However, before doing so he decided to consult Rabbi Menachem Mendel. To his consternation, Rabbi Menachem Mendel explained to him the Mishna and proved that the traditional text contained no error. Rabbi Isaac Meir then said: "There is no doubt in my mind that the *tanna* who was the author of that Mishna taught its meaning to Rabbi Menachem Mendel. It is beyond the power of a human being to achieve such understanding on his own."[3]

Unlike all other great scholars of all generations who found fulfillment in writing books, Rabbi Menachem Mendel aspired instead to convert scholarship into a tool with which to raise great personalities. He abhorred writing, which was to him a sheer waste of time. He explained this unwillingness to put his thoughts in print:

> Let us suppose that I have already written a book. Who will buy it? Some of our people. And when will our people find time to read a book, when they are so busy making a living all week long? Surely, on the Sabbath. However, on the Sabbath, they must take a ritual bath and then pray, and later on eat their Sabbath meal; only after the meal will they be free to read. They will stretch out on the couch, open the book, and be ready to read it. But let us not forget that when people are full they start drowsing and the book will fall out of their hands. Now tell me, do I have to write a book in order to put people to sleep?[4]

This is a typical Kotzker story. Its author could not make peace with the fact that man has to labor six days and only the seventh is left for the elevation of the soul. But even then, earthly concerns interfere with man's desire to raise himself above the commonplace.

As time went on and his habits of thinking settled in definite patterns, Rabbi Menachem Mendel developed an all-embracing concept of study in which there was no room left for any other human concern. The study of Torah demanded the entire man.

The words "You and all your house come into the ark" (Genesis 7:1) meant to the Kotzker: "Enter (into the pursuit of Torah) with all your body and soul." This was what the Sages had in mind when they said: "When a man professes that he has labored hard to understand the Torah, believe him" (Megillah 6). When a man labors hard and makes a sincere effort, only then will he attain an understanding of the Torah. Those who do not do their utmost, and still pride themselves that they know, will forget their knowledge just as easily as it was attained.[5]

"But his delight is in the Torah of God" (Psalms 1:2) — This verse meant to the Kotzker that the student who only takes delight in his study but does not put his mind to work will ultimately fail to understand the Torah. Knowledge of Torah can be achieved neither by piety nor by prayer, but through "the exercise of reason and logic."[6] "A man of learning is superior to a prophet" (Baba Bathra 12), and therefore we should learn how to live as Jews only from the devoted students of the Torah.[7]

The ways of Torah study are preferable to the ways of chasiduth. Even Rabbi Israel Ba'al Shem Tov, the founder of chasiduth, who taught his followers a new way of worshiping God, did not consider this new way superior to the ways of Torah. The teachings of the Ba'al Shem Tov were necessary because the study of Torah had deteriorated in his generation and the rabbis explained the Torah improperly. Chasiduth, therefore, restored the upset balance. However, under ordinary circumstances, the ways of Torah study are more desirable than the ways of chasiduth.[8]

The Rabbi of Kotzk was thus caught in a web of contradictions. His logical radicalism prompted him to upset the balance between Torah and *avoda* (Divine worship). The entire structure of Jewish life was built upon the saying of Simon the Just, who taught: "Upon three things the world is based: upon the Torah, upon Divine service, and upon the practice of charity" (Aboth 1:2). These three fundamentals were regarded as equally important on the Jewish scale of values, and Divine service was never thought of as an obstacle to Torah. However, the Rabbi of Kotzk tipped the scale in the direction of Torah. Rabbi Abraham of Sochatzev quoted Rabbi Menachem Mendel as having told him, "You, Abraham, are great in prayer, and I am afraid that this might harm your power of reasoning."[9]

This scaling down of prayer was a modification of his previous stand. At one time Rabbi Menachem Mendel taught his adherents: "The men who are great in the study of Torah supplement the work of the men who busy themselves with Divine worship; they help one another. And if one is incomplete, the other is incomplete too."[10]

A story was told about a chasid who complained to the Kotzker that he found it exceedingly hard to earn a living. The rabbi counseled him to pray to God with all his heart and the Lord would have mercy on him. The chasid then declared that he did not know how to pray. Rabbi Menachem Mendel looked at the chasid with much concern, and told him: "You are the victim of an affliction greater than the worry about a livelihood; you must learn how to give utterance to prayer."[11]

In the following story we find the same attitude towards prayer.

A chasid frequently interjected in his prayers the exclamation: "Father, O Father." A second chasid found fault with this manner of prayer and quoted the Talmud: "When we obey God, He is called our Father; otherwise, He is our Master" (Kiddushin 36).

"What gives this man the right to regard himself as worthy enough to call God his Father and not his Master?" he later inquired.

To this Rabbi Menachem Mendel remarked: "If one cries out 'Father, O Father' many times, at last God becomes in truth his Father."[12]

To the Rabbi of Kotzk, prayer was much more than a mere rendering into words of some prayerbook passages. Real prayer meant a state of feeling in which the soul divested itself of its corporality and reached unison with its Maker. Once, he remarked that "in prayer one goes from the lower into the higher spheres and back into the lower, like a captain who directs his ship from crest to ebb."[13] And still, he did not reject mere "mechanical" prayer. When a chasid complained before him that he did not feel himself closer to God when he prayed, the Kotzker replied: "You should not be concerned about this. Prayer is very important, and when you pray once with devotion, this prayer will bring up before the Heavenly Throne all the preceding prayers that you uttered without devotion."[14]

The verse "He will fulfill the desire of those who fear Him; He will also hear their cry" (Psalms 145:19) he interpreted to mean: "God craves the prayers of the righteous and, therefore, He fulfills their desires in order that they pray to Him."[15]

How can we reconcile these contradictory attitudes towards prayer? On the one hand, we see a complete acceptance of prayer and an affirmation of its importance; on the other, an apprehension that prayer (and observance) might prevent the achievement of mastery in the study of Torah.

114

A partial solution to this paradox might be provided by stating that the Rabbi of Kotzk drew the most far-reaching conclusions from each premise he was preoccupied with. When he dealt with prayer, he exhausted all possibilities inherent in this presupposition; and when he dwelt upon Torah, he reached the most radical conclusions conceivable.

However, it is hard to accept that Rabbi Menachem Mendel, who possessed a sharp mind and a clear-thinking head, was entrapped in a logical labyrinth of his own making. All the sayings and different stories preserved by chasidic tradition are not dated, and it is impossible for us to pinpoint the exact stage of his development to which they belong. It is the opinion here that Rabbi Menachem Mendel's critical attitude towards prayer presents a later development in his life, when his mind was troubled with many thoughts and doubts which he was unable to resolve.

The disregard for the "golden mean" and the noted preference for the extreme was manifested also in the Kotzker system of ethics. "Take heed to yourselves that you go not up onto the mount or touch the border of it" (Exodus 19:12) meant according to Rabbi Menachem Mendel: "The one who goes up should take heed not to be satisfied with merely touching the border; he should reach the top of the mount."[16] And so he moved from his previous position of acceptance of temporal life to a complete denial of it.

The same man who once resolved that King Solomon was the wisest of men because he taught us, through the institutions he established, to associate with people and to separate from them when needed — the same Rabbi Menachem Mendel of Kotzk now reached completely different conclusions. "In the entire existence of the universe there is no existence besides the existence of God, and all that man sees with his eyes of flesh has no existence at all."[17]

The Rabbi of Kotzk had thus reached a position where everything had to be holy in its entirety and completely "for the sake of Heaven," without any concessions to the demands and needs of the profane. He concluded that "The pursuance of the ways of the Torah is the greatest chastisement of the body." When a man fulfills the commandments of God, "he gives himself away fully."[18] "The righteous should become completely righteous, even though this might make the wicked completely wicked." When our forefather Jacob told his family, "Put away the strange gods that are among you" (Genesis 35:2), he forbade them to enjoy even the bodily pleasures that are permissible, but do not make for holiness.[19]

Rabbi Menachem Mendel thus reached the end of the road on which he was traveling. He put on the faithful flock of his chasidim exaggerated demands that could hardly be followed, even by the best and most dedicated of them. He asserted that he needed excellent men with whom he could share his opinions, and not a herd which had eyes for things material. He refused to see the throngs that flocked to his residence and craved his advice and blessings; many of the petitioners were met by a harangue of abuse and slander. "What do you want from me, you horses, oxen? I need chasidim and not cattle!" To the small group of his most trusted disciples, he complained: "I thought that only four hundred select men will follow me; I will lead them into the forest and supply them with *manna* from heaven and they will come to know His kingdom."[20]

The daily routine of a chasidic rabbi put him in a state of rage and exhaustion. Unable to bear the countless demands of the petitioning chasidim, he lost all patience for their tales about family and daily concerns. He locked himself in his room and refused to see anybody. Then he would unexpectedly open the door of the study, look at the assembled crowd, and utter angrily a few sentences of denunciation. A dreadful reverence would overtake the awestruck crowd; they would listen frantically to the rabbi's words, and then suddenly start running away through all the doors and windows.

Once, he appeared at the door of the house of study and shouted at the assembled students: "You expect to become rabbis? Your flesh will be consumed by vermin before you achieve this!" The frightened chasidim fled in panic in order not to listen to their rabbi's curses, because they staunchly believed that every word of his would be fulfilled.[21]

After the death in 1838 of Rabbi Menachem Mendel's first wife, Glike, he remarried. This was due to the insistence of his most trusted disciple, Rabbi Isaac Meir. His second wife was Chaya, the sister-in-law of Rabbi Isaac Meir. According to chasidic legend, the bride's sister, Rabbi Isaac Meir's wife, came to Kotzk and demanded from the rabbi an assurance that her sister would bear children from him, "children who will busy themselves with Torah and the commandments." The rabbi promised her that he "will lead the children to their wedding canopy" — a promise that he fulfilled in the years to come.

After his second marriage, the Kotzker Rabbi mellowed considerably. He became more sociable and more accessible to his chasidim. To the delight of his faithful followers, he again took a sympathetic interest in their problems, and lavishly dispensed words of counsel and consolation. He was virtually besieged by masses of chasidim and people in distress, and he tried to be helpful to everybody. The downtrodden and the deranged were especially close to his heart, and many beautiful stories are told about the ways he provided them with a spiritual uplift.

However, with the passage of time, the Kotzker Rabbi drifted back to his former habits of seclusion and disinterest in all human concerns. He was again lonesome and submerged in study and contemplation; only rarely did he agree to see his chasidim and talk to them. For weeks, the faithful, who came from afar to see him, waited in vain for the farewell blessing which was not forthcoming. When, in their despair, they approached him to ask for permission to leave, words of abuse and denunciations were heaped on them. The anguish of the chasidim was unbearable. In their despondency, some left on their own, while others remained, still hoping a change for the better would take place.

The Rabbi of Kotzk seemed to be completely insensitive to the sorrow and grief of his chasidim. For many months he walked about as if in a trance, absorbed entirely in his own thoughts, his eyes flashing fire and his entire being vibrating with secrecy. Everyone sensed that a gale was gathering force within him, but nobody knew when it would burst forth and how it would end. His family sensed that something was wrong, for in recent nights he had paced his room like a caged lion, sometimes growling and roaring loudly.

They immediately sent for his intimate chasid and friend, Rabbi Mordecai Joseph Leiner, and asked him to stay and relieve Rabbi Menachem Mendel's loneliness. When Mordecai Joseph came, on a Friday, the Kotzker refused to receive him and only towards evening did he ask Mordecai Joseph to go out for a walk in the woods. The men walked side by side for a long time without a word being uttered by either one. The silence was finally broken by Rabbi Mordecai Joseph, who remarked to the master that they might have strayed too far and thus violated the laws governing Sabbath observance.

It is difficult to know definitely what troubled Rabbi Menachem Mendel and what preoccupied his distressed mind. But chasidic tradition relates that upon hearing Rabbi Mordecai Joseph's remark his face became clouded, his eyes grew sadder than ever before, and a deep oppressive sorrow enveloped his entire being.[23]

In this depressed state of mind the Rabbi of Kotzk returned home to the trembling household and chasidim who fearfully awaited the future. For many hours he remained in his room, refusing to see anybody. At about midnight, he emerged from his solitude, shaking and trembling. He went to the table, took a glass of wine, and kept it in the palm of his hand. He remained as motionless as a pillar of marble. It was quite evident that a mighty conflict was raging within him, and all trembled at the sight of his face.

Instead of chanting the *kiddush*, he apparently said some words which sounded like blasphemy to the surrounding chasidim — or at least to some of them. What really transpired in Kotzk on that eventful Sabbath Eve cannot be determined. We have many conflicting reports, and all of them are tinged with subjectivity and partiality.

The chasidim of Kozenitz, who were opposed to Rabbi Menachem Mendel's system, maintained that he had lost his senses. The *maskilim* announced victoriously that the Rabbi of Kotzk had denied the existence of God by proclaiming, "There is no judgment and there is no Judge" (Bereshith Rabba 26).

The most popularly accepted report alleges that the Kotzker hurled the glass away, extinguished the candles, and exclaimed, in a bitter and fearful voice: "Get out of here, imbeciles, I am neither your rabbi nor the son of a rabbi!"

The dumbfounded chasidim did not know what to make of this event. The ones whose belief in their master was unlimited remained faithful to him and attributed to this shocking event a mystical meaning. Others became frightened and ran away in utter confusion. The only one who retained the courage to remonstrate with his master was Rabbi Mordecai Joseph Leiner, who repudiated the teachings of Rabbi Menachem Mendel and walked out with all the secessionists. Rabbi Mordecai Joseph supposedly issued the call, "Whosoever is for God, follow me" (Exodus 32:26).[24]

Among the secessionists who followed Rabbi Mordecai Joseph, the founder of the Izbitza system, were many important Kotzker chasidim. However, some of them, overtaken by longings, returned to Rabbi Menachem Mendel later on. The antagonism between the two systems of chasiduth, Kotzk and Izbitza, outlived the lives of their founders and continued for many years. Some even believed that this split in the ranks of the chasidim caused a delay in the coming of the Messianic Age, which was to commence in the year 1840, according to the Zohar.[25]

After this tragic incident, which took place in 1839, Rabbi Menachem Mendel locked himself in his room, cut himself off from the tide of life, and remained in self-imposed confinement for twenty years, until his death in 1859. His immediate family members and faithful followers, who desired to rescue what still could be salvaged from the flock of chasidim, explained that the light emanating from the tzaddik was very great and blinded the eyes, and that his flame was scorching hot; therefore, the world could not stand his presence. It was better, then, that the strong light be confined and isolated from the rest of the world. However, even from the place of his isolation, the Rabbi of Kotzk would be gracious enough to procure great benefits and blessings for the faithful of his chasidim.[26]

A distant echo of the unusual event of that fateful Friday night in 1839 is found in a letter written about half-a-year later by the faithful Rabbi Isaac Meir to another Kotzker chasid, Rabbi Eleazar HaCohen. The people who spread the false rumors are called "cursed arrogants." The letter reads:

> In the evening I received your letter. I was in Kotzk last Sabbath and found everything to be all right, thanks to God. He (the rabbi) spent three Sabbaths with the crowd. The rumors were probably spread by cursed arrogants, whose eyes ache, as if touched with itching thorns, at the sight of men who accept the Torah of God.[27]

The mere fact that the calm and levelheaded Rabbi Isaac Meir found such strong language necessary in denouncing the rumors points to their popularity, and their dangerous connotations for the good name of Kotzk.

Chapter 8 — Notes

1. *Emet V'Emuna,* par. 677
2. *Emet V'Emuna,* par. 859
3. *Amud Ha'Emet,* p. 107
4. Ehrlich, *l. c.,* p. 35
5. *Amud Ha'Emet,* p. 7; *Ohel Torah,* par. 208
6. *Emet V'Emuna,* par. 622; *Ohel Torah,* par. 232

7. *Emet V'Emuna,* par. 204; *Amud Ha'Emet,* p. 87
8. *Abir HaRoim,* par. 110
9. *Abir HaRoim,* par. 37
10. *Emet V'Emuna,* p. 197
11. Ehrlich, *l. c.,* p. 38
12. *Emet V'Emuna,* par. 85
13. *Abir HaRoim,* par. 49
14. *Emet V'Emuna,* par. 8
15. *Ohel Torah,* par. 260
16. *Amud Ha'Emet,* p. 24
17. *Amud Ha'Emet,* p. 61, p. 44
18. *Emet V'Emuna,* par. 51, par. 23
19. *Amud Ha'Emet,* p. 7, p. 10
20. *Emet V'Emuna,* par. 145
21. *Emet V'Emuna,* par. 664; *Abir HaRoim,* par. 43
22. Gliksman, *l. c.,* pp. 47-52
23. Elzet, Yehuda, *Kotzk,* in *Mizrachi;* No. 67, Warsaw 1920
24. Gliksman, *l. c.,* chapter 14
25. *Siach Sarfey Kodesh,* vol. 2, p. 5
26. *Meir Eyney Hagola,* vol. 1, p. 94
27. *Meir Eyney Hagola,* par. 359

Chapter 9

The Years of Confinement

The illusive event of the fateful Sabbath Eve in 1839 casts its shadow over the entire Kotzk story. Though we do not know exactly what took place, it is clear that this episode marks the culmination in the inner development of Rabbi Menachem Mendel. On this climactic Friday night, the usually tight-mouthed Rabbi Menachem Mendel uttered some words that he was unable to contain within himself any longer. He thus gave away his thoughts, the conclusions of years of solitary thinking, and expressed his innermost convictions. The Rabbi of Kotzk knew that his chasidim were not ready to share with him these ideas. However, so obsessed was he with this truth that he could no longer suppress it; in spite of his better judgment, he felt compelled to speak before an audience that was not prepared for it. The reaction to this revelation was so shocking that for the remaining twenty years of his life he shut himself off from the outside world and lived in voluntary confinement.

Had chasidic tradition preserved for us the exact words of the Kotzker on that eventful Friday night, the enigma of Kotzk would have been solved. However, chasidic tradition preferred to keep silent on this point. The chasidim, who never tired of repeating their rabbi's praises and teachings, were usually silent and noncommittal when it came to shedding some light on this episode. They surely wanted to blot out this painful event from their memories and make posterity forget it.

Even if we concede the point to the chasidic writers that all this was pure fabrication, invented and exploited by the Kotzker's numerous enemies in other chasidic courts, our analysis of the Kotzk system would have to continue in the same way. There is no escaping the fact that the Rabbi of Kotzk was tired of life, disgusted with his chasidim, and inclined to live in isolation. For this we have the testimony of Aaron Walden, a contemporary rabbinic author who visited Rabbi Menachem Mendel and wrote about him in flowering terms. In his encyclopedia of Jewish celebrities he records:

> And after his heart comprehended fully the ways of God, our holy rabbi chose to be separated from people, and he lived in isolation. For about twenty years, his feet did not step outside the confines of his house. And he continued to grow in purity and sanctity and his Torah utterances won wide acclaim.[1]

This makes it clear that his confinement was an undisputed fact. Now it remains for us to reconstruct the state of mind that forced him into this situation, and to trace the ideas he entertained that made him the misunderstood man he was.

His life during the period of isolation was tragic, and every word he uttered attested to his spiritual sufferings. "He who increases knowledge, his knowledge increases his pain" (Ecclesiastes 1:18). "A man must always strive to increase his knowledge, even though his pain is increased," said Rabbi Menachem Mendel.[2]

No one was permitted to enter his room. Only on the most extraordinary occasions were a few of his closest intimates allowed to see him. There were times when he burst forth from his

124

room into the large chamber and screamed at those who were sitting there. His greatest disciple, Rabbi Isaac Meir, with the help of Rabbi Menachem Mendel's son, Rabbi David, would then soothe him until he returned to his study, where he paced back and forth like a caged lion. On one occasion, Rabbi Yechiel Meir, later the tzaddik from Gostinin, carried Rabbi Menachem Mendel on his shoulder to his chamber; at other times, Yechiel Meir's young wife, Hershia, would come in and quiet him.[3]

Moments of grace were few. On those occasions he would chat with those closest to him, and sometimes on a Sabbath morning he would give a discourse to the assembled chasidim. The old chasidim related that there were two entrances from the rabbi's room facing the *beth hamidrash*. All week they were padlocked; on the Sabbath and holidays one pair of doors would be opened, and in the other pair would be two large holes through which the rabbi heard the public worship, and occasionally peeped through them. His grandsons would enter his chamber every Saturday and he would examine them on what they had studied during the week; afterwards he would distribute fruit to them.

When loneliness overwhelmed him, he would tremble, assail and break window panes, curse, and pour abuse and insults. No man would then escape his wrath. After awhile, when the rabbi's anger subsided, he became even sadder, as he convinced himself that nobody needed him — not even his trusted chasidim. After the secession of Rabbi Mordecai Joseph Leiner, he suspected everybody of treason. When Rabbi Isaac Meir, in his travels, visited, in Sadigora, Rabbi Israel of Rizhin, the arch enemy of Kotzk, Rabbi Menachem Mendel harbored in his heart misgivings even about him. Rabbi Isaac Meir was then compelled to assure Rabbi Menachem Mendel of his loyalty and declare that he found nothing in Sadigora that could not be found in Kotzk.[4]

Many of the chasidim who in the first fit of resentment followed the rebellion of Rabbi Mordecai Joseph Leiner were overcome by their yearnings and started to drift back to Kotzk. With bowed heads and dormant hopes that they would be granted forgiveness, they stood shamefacedly before the door that led to Rabbi Menachem Mendel's quarters. However, their rabbi showed no sympathy for the weaknesses of human nature. "Why did you return and who asked you?" he thundered at them. "Do you think that I am a chimney sweep [of souls]?" At another time he was reported to have told one of his renowned followers who deserted him and came back later: "You should revere your rabbi as you revere the heavens (Aboth 4:15). Tell me, are there two heavens?"[5]

This utterance may provide us with an opportunity to explore Rabbi Menachem Mendel's opinion about himself. What was his self-image and what importance did he ascribe to his person and his teachings? Chasidic tradition preserved for us many sayings of his which might give us useful clues as to the Kotzker's thoughts about himself and the mission he had to fulfill.

It was already mentioned that the Rabbi of Kotzk referred to himself as "a good Jew." He explained that a rabbi of chasidim was called by that appellation "because he is select and good throughout." There are two kinds of Jews: Jews of lesser and of higher quality. This he deduced from the verse in the book of Psalms: "Blow ye the trumpet on the new moon, in the time appointed, on our solemn feast day. For it is a law for Israel, an ordinance of the God of Jacob" (Psalms 81:4, 5). The designation "Israel" is attributed here to the men of importance and prominence, to the great tzaddikim to whom this is law. But the people called by the name "Jacob," the people of lesser quality, to them this is an ordinance.[6]

What are the characteristics of a "tzaddik"? Once he started to expound: "I render thanks to Thee (the prayer uttered when awakening in the morning), who am I?" Chasidic tradition relates that the rabbi stopped here and did not explain any further. However, what he was reluctant to disclose in public, he revealed in private to his son-in-law, Rabbi Abraham of Sochatzev, who wrote: "His holy soul dates back to the times before the destruction of the Temple, and his coming to this world was for the sake of clarification of what is holiness and what is exterior form." On another occasion: "Once he said that he does not need the intercession of angels to carry his prayers to the Heavenly Throne. His prayers reach the heavens directly." And about the chasidim he said: "They are not in a position to evaluate what a rabbi they have."[7]

The Kotzker knew that he exerted a profound influence on his chasidim. He said: "I straighten them out, and when they come to me the second time, I cannot recognize them anymore. And what more could the Messiah accomplish? . . . Every soul must come to me, to Kotzk, for salvation, even if it is behind the Mountains of Darkness . . . I could, if only I wanted, bring the dead back to life, but my purpose is to keep the living alive."[8]

None of his disciples doubted even for a moment that he was invested with supernatural powers. Rabbi Yechiel Meir of Gostinin said once: "When he was swaying in prayer, all the world swayed together with him . . . with a word of his he could resurrect the dead." Once he expounded before his assembled chasidim the Midrashic portion pertaining to the weekly Scriptural reading, and when he read the phrase: "I am the Owner of the Citadel" (Bereshith Rabba 39), all the trembling chasidim felt that they had experienced the presence of God. It was an accepted practice for the Kotzker chasidim to say: "Our rabbi's greeting is like the story of creation, his farewell — like Ezekiel's vision of God's chariot."[9]

The clearest indication about his concept of himself is contained in the following story: In a loud voice he said to one of his chasidim, "Do you know who I am? (Seven generations had passed since the time of Rabbi Israel Ba'al Shem Tov.) There was Rabbi Dov Ber, after him came Rabbi Shmelke, and then Rabbi Elimelech; he was followed by the Rabbi of Lublin and then came HaYehudi, and later Rabbi Simcha Bunim; and I am the seventh; I am the quintessence of all of them. I am the Sabbath."[10]

When stripped of their mystical overtones, all these quotations give us a clear indication about Rabbi Menachem Mendel's assumed mission in life. He was the seventh in the line of succession after Israel Ba'al Shem Tov, the founder of chasiduth. And as the seventh day of the week brought tranquility and holiness to men, so was it his duty to cure the chasidic movement from all its shortcomings and restore it to a state of perfection. Rabbi Israel Ba'al Shem Tov did not spend his energy on the writing of books, but on the cultivation of great personalities. Likewise, Rabbi Menachem Mendel's highest aspiration was to surround himself with followers who personified the Jewish ideal of perfection. In order to achieve perfection, he had to clarify "what was holiness and what was exterior form." The rationalist within him could not accept the hallowed-by-tradition Jewish way of life at face value. Understanding and meaningful experience meant to him more than the emphasis on the minutiae of observance. The Kotzker was years ahead of his time, and even his most faithful followers could not understand him. This gave rise to a whole series of misunderstandings that culminated in Rabbi Menachem Mendel's voluntary isolation.

Chasidic tradition has transmitted to posterity a number of odd-sounding stories which picture the Rabbi of Kotzk as a rebel who infringed on the customary tenets of Jewish observance. These stories tie in nicely with his non-conformist pronouncements quoted in the former chapter.

A curious visitor once asked the Kotzker when the latter observed the customary midnight ceremonial of mourning for the destruction of the Temple (*Tikkun Chatzot*), since he saw the rabbi eating around midnight. To this the Kotzker replied: When I include in my after-meal grace the petition: "Rebuild Jerusalem, the holy city," I observe the midnight mourning for the Temple.

Another story relates that a pauper, who was a guest at the rabbi's Passover table, drank the wine from Elijah the Prophet's cup. The rabbi told the embarrassed guest: "Do not feel guilty; if Elijah, who is also a guest at this table, did not empty his cup, you have done well in drinking for him."[11]

We do not know in what period of his life these incidents occurred. However, the stories related below happened during the period of his confinement. Two of them are connected with the observance of Passover.

Once, when the entire household and the close chasidim sat down for the Passover supper (*Seder*), the rabbi did not distribute the customary bitter herbs (*maror*) during the Seder ritual. The chasidim whispered to Rabbi Abraham of Sochatzev to remind the rabbi of this oversight. Rabbi Abraham then mentioned a controversy as to the source for the introduction of *maror*. Some claimed that it was of Biblical origin, while others insisted it was rabbinic; however, he maintained it was Biblical.

Rabbi Menachem Mendel told him, "You are right," and gave *maror* to everybody. Then suddenly his mood changed and he began to shout: "*maror* gulpers." The scared guests ran away from the table; only Rabbi Abraham remained. Rabbi Menachem Mendel turned to him and asked for a comment on the subject of Passover. He listened with unusual interest to his son-in-law's discourse. His eyes twinkled with sparks of fire and he seemed to be completely divested from earthly concerns.

Then Rabbi Hirsch Tomashover, the manager of the household, reentered and the Kotzker Rabbi asked him: "Where are all the people?" Rabbi Hirsch reminded him that they were driven away when he shouted "*maror* gulpers." The Kotzker Rabbi replied that he did not mean them.[12]

The next episode is even more revealing. As the rabbi observed the second Seder by himself in his room, the chasidim waited in the adjoining hall for his appearance, when he would open the door to recite the passage: "Pour out your wrath . . ." The rabbi, feeling the anxiety of his chasidim, opened the door and mocked them: "The rabbi 'poured' already at this door or at another door; the printer printed — and they follow him; would it please him to print something else, they would have acted differently. Everything depends on the printer's whims and moods."[13]

These occurrences, when combined with the other utterances, reveal a mind that is impatient with the slavish observance of the minutiae of ritual. The Rabbi of Kotzk seemingly objected to narrowing down Jewishness to a detailed list of motions that must follow one another. To him, many of these were trivial and irrelevant. His protest against overstressing the incidental and inconsequential is expressed at times good-naturedly, at other times angrily and sarcastically.

Did the Rabbi of Kotzk conclude that the rituals, or some of them, are not necessarily an expression of the spirit of Judaism, but are only a manifestation of it? It is, therefore, more important to keep the spirit alive than the mere expressions of it. He might have noticed that the emphasis upon all the details of ritual tends to weaken the essence. As a mystic, he regarded the inner experience of perceiving Judaism's historical and metaphysical quality as much more important than merely following a prescribed course of actions that did not necessarily make for spirituality. He looked with contempt at the petty characters who converted the soul-stirring verities into a stereotyped course of action. The printer printed — and they follow him; would it please the printer to print something else, they would have acted differently.

As the man who was supposed to bring the teachings of the Ba'al Shem to their final perfection, he desired a chasiduth that was pure, distilled essence, purged of all the non-essential. His soul dated back to hallowed antiquity and, therefore, he was invested with the authority to introduce changes in the code of laws. "I am presiding over the seventy members of the Sanhedrin and it is within my power to allow the sounding of the *shofar* on the Sabbath, in accordance with the decision of Maimonides."[14]

It was an accepted chasidic axiom that "the tzaddik decrees and God puts the decree into effect" (Rabbi Elimelech). In keeping within this line of thought, the Kotzker explained Maimonides' opinion that spirits do not have any real existence, though in the Talmud the existence of spirits is mentioned many times. In olden times there were spirits; however, when Maimonides decided that they did not exist, it was decided so in the heavens, too.[15] And the same right to arrive at decisions that would be acceptable to the heavens Rabbi Menachem Mendel claimed for himself as well.

In the year 1851, the Russian government decreed that the Jews must give up their special garb and dress like all the other inhabitants of the empire. To the observant Jews this was a severe blow to their way of life. Rabbi Isaac Meir evoked a Talmudic rule: "Be killed and do not transgress" (Pesachim 25), and recommended a mass movement of non-compliance with the law. This irked the Rabbi of Kotzk, who was at this point in sharp disagreement with almost all the Polish rabbis. He did not regard the peculiar Polish Jewish attire as an essential part of Judaism. "There is no need to be killed for a suit of clothing," he explained.[16]

From all that has been said about Rabbi Menachem Mendel's opposition to an overemphasis on ritual, we should in no way construe his attitude as opposition to all rituals. "Once he asked Rabbi Chanoch HaCohen to study the problem of eating soaked *matzah* on Passover. Upon the completion of his research, Rabbi Chanoch concluded that he found no objection to allowing the consumption of soaked *matzah*. To this the Kotzker replied that the custom of abstaining from soaked *matzah* must have some mystical meaning and should be continued."[17]

No matter how subjectively justified were Rabbi Menachem Mendel's ideas, we can readily understand the embarrassment and bewilderment of his chasidim. They did not go through the same process of agonizing thought and careful examination of all the fundamentals of Judaism as their rabbi had done. Little did they know about all the gnawing doubts and perplexing questions that robbed their leader of his peace of mind, making him the perplexing man he was to them. No wonder, therefore, that they were shocked when he came up with answers and statements that were far beyond their comprehension. Friendly and unfriendly chasidim alike, *mithnagdim* and secularists — all were astounded, and were unable to comprehend what had happened to the Rabbi of Kotzk. This misunderstanding gave rise to different stories and rumors, which added to the confusion surrounding the personality of Rabbi Menachem Mendel. The entire concept of ritual as an aspect of Judaism, and not as its essence, was far beyond the grasp of his generation.

Little wonder that the Rabbi of Kotzk preferred the solitude of his room to the company of chasidim. He did not need their admiration; all he wanted was understanding, and this he could not attain. "Soon they will proclaim me to be a deity, but I am a broken and imperfect man."[18] If for a time he lived with the illusion that all he had to do was to tell his chasidim what he was thinking about, and they would follow him, the events of the tragic Friday night in 1839 convinced him that this was not the case. It was quite feasible to assume that his confinement was an enforced one, at least at the beginning. His family and entourage did not want his chasidim to hear ideas they were incapable of understanding; otherwise, his chasidim would surely be driven away from the camp of Kotzk.

He lived on a different plane than all the people around him. Never too interested in ordinary human affairs, he now cut off his contacts with the outside world entirely. When told that there was a famine in the land and that many people walked around hungry, his reply was: "I am not afraid of the famine, but I am deeply concerned with the cruelty that resides in the hearts of men." He constantly complained that the world was infested with a bad stench which was impossible for him to bear. "Once I thought that

I would be able to overcome the stench and the forces of impurity, the falsehood and the make-believe, but I was badly beaten."[19]

Only rarely did he allow anyone to enter his room; hardly ever did he walk out to show himself to the few faithful who waited for him outside. When he began to lose his eyesight and the doctors recommended eyeglasses, he refused to take their advice. "He did not want to put a barrier between his eyes and the holy Torah."[20] According to chasidic tradition, he spent many sleepless nights towards the end of his life writing a one-page volume which was supposed to contain his entire philosophy. Entitling it *Torath Adam* (Teachings for Man), he wrote and rewrote it many times and finally ordered it burned, together with all his other manuscripts.

He died, unreconciled with the world, in 1859. His chasidim attached importance to the fact that their rabbi was called to his Maker on the week when the Scriptural words "And to Moses He said, go up to God" (Exodus 24:1) was read in the synagogue. Rabbi Isaac Meir of Ger, who was regarded as his spiritual heir, eulogized him: " 'The tzaddik passed away and no man puts it to heart' (Isaiah 57:1) — there is no other man left to put the Torah into the heart of the people, as did Rabbi Menachem Mendel!"[21]

Chapter 9 — Notes

.. Walden, Aaron, *Shem HaGedolim,* quoted from Ehrlich, *l. c.,* p. 40
2. *Amud Ha'Emet,* p. 59
3. *Meir Eyney Hagola,* v. 1, p. 69
4. *Meir Eyney Hagola,* v. 1, p. 378
5. *Amud Ha'Emet,* p. 115

6. *Amud Ha'Emet,* p. 91; *Ohel Torah,* p. 248
7. *Emet V'Emuna,* par. 647; *Abir HaRoim,* p. 49
8. *Emet V'Emuna,* par. 728; *Siach Sarfey Kodesh,* p. 131; *Amud Ha'Emet,* p. 89
9. *Emet V'Emuna,* par. 128, par. 871; *Siach,* p. 185
10. *Emet V'Emuna,* par. 906
11. *Amud Ha'Emet,* p. 95; *Arigur, l. c.,* p. 109
12. *Emet V'Emuna,* par. 873
13. *Arigur, l. c.,* p. 109
14. *Amud Ha'Emet,* p. 76
15. *Amud Ha'Emet,* p. 67
16. *Emet V'Emuna,* par. 140, p. 270
17. *Emet V'Emuna,* par. 841
18. *Arigur, l. c.,* p. 90
19. *Arigur, l. c.,* p. 102
20. *Emet V'Emuna,* par. 783
21. *Amud Ha'Emet,* p. 102

Chapter 10

Sayings of the Kotzker

The Man

The sayings of Rabbi Menachem Mendel were many. At times
they were spoken in deep bitterness, at other times with deep
compassion and humility. The mood he was in or his state of mind
was the guide to these variations.

In attempting to achieve the desired comprehension and
apprehension of the Divine, Rabbi Menachem Mendel often
worried over man's logical comprehensions of God; after the
passing of "The Holy Jew," he took on another worry: Who
would his teacher be?

Then one night, in a vision or dream, "The Holy Jew"
appeared before him and tried to console him, saying, "I will
continue to serve you as teacher!" Rabbi Menachem Mendel
listened, and then replied: "I do not want a teacher from the
hereafter."

Rabbi Menachem Mendel, during the years he spent in
Peshischa, was very poor. Never in all those years did he have a
penny in his pocket. He was always dressed in tattered rags. It
didn't seem to bother him; in fact, he was very seldom even aware
of his dire circumstance.

When Tamar, the known benefactoress of the chasidim, visited

Peshischa, Rabbi Feivel, a very dear and close friend of Rabbi Menachem Mendel's, attempted to persuade the latter to improve his dress and do away with ragged clothes. Rabbi Feivel said to him, "Have a look at the tattered rags you wear. Tamar is kind; she has arrived here and will help. Go to her and let her give you the money for some new clothes, a new suit."

Rabbi Menachem Mendel, looking at him wearily and contemptuously, answered, "What? Money?" Then, in violent anger, he spat bitterly into the air.

Rabbi Feivel was astonished and taken aback in horror. Later, when recalling this incident, he could only express his feelings by saying, "For thirty days after this conversation, whenever I saw money or it was mentioned, I can assure you I turned sick; my intestines seemed to turn upside down."

Rabbi Menachem Mendel was very witty, and often surprised his chasidim with droll remarks. Once when he entered the house of study he announced, "I am a great man of learning; I am a great man of learning." The chasidim looked at him in amazement. Then he went on to explain: "I am a disciple of Rabbi Simcha Bunim of Peshischa, who was a man of great learning." (*Talmid Chacham*, "scholar," literally means "student of a scholar.")

Rabbi Menachem Mendel called together all the young among his chasidim, and told them: "I want you not to sin — not because it is forbidden to sin, but because you should never have free time available for sinning."

The erratic actions of Rabbi Menachem Mendel were varied. Once Rabbi Yechiel Meir, the future Rabbi of Gostinin, rushed into Rabbi Menachem Mendel's study, his face beaming, and in a voice of great joy exclaimed, "Rabbi, I won a lot of money." (Rabbi Yechiel Meir was known for his great poverty.)

Rabbi Menachem Mendel, in turn, fearing that he was being accused of performing a miracle, grabbed him by his collar and dragged him out, shouting, "I am not guilty of it, I am not guilty of it."

In dismay, Rabbi Yechiel Meir rushed home, called together all of his needy colleagues, and gave away all the money that he had.

It was not unusual for Rabbi Menachem Mendel to speak harshly of others. Once he criticized one of the well-known chasidic rebbes. When the latter heard about it, he immediately sent a message to the Rabbi of Kotzk. "Do you known how great I am? My greatness reaches the seventh heaven."

Without hesitation and with a great deal of candor, Rabbi Menachem Mendel replied: "I am so small that all the seven heavens bend down to me."

Very shortly after this incident a chasid came to the Rabbi of Kotzk and asked for a blessing. During the conversation the man informed the rabbi that because of old age he had given up his trade, and now his children refused to provide for him. He lamented that all the years of his life he had worked and provided unstintingly for the children; now, when he had become aged, they refused to take an interest in him or give him any assistance.

Rabbi Menachem Mendel remained silent. Meditating for awhile, he then raised his head, opened his eyes, and whispered, "That is what it is. The father is perturbed by the sorrows of his children, but the children are not at all moved by the sorrows of the father."

A story is told about the time a chasid who was an adherent of a different rebbe came to visit Rabbi Menachem Mendel of Kotzk. During his visit the rabbi asked him, "What does your rebbe do?"

The chasid pondered for a moment and then replied, "They tell that my rebbe can perform miracles."

Rabbi Menachem Mendel looked at the chasid and then spoke. "Miracles? This doesn't matter very much to me. What does matter is: Can he perform the miracle of taking a man from the street and making him a chasid? This is a miracle."

We are told that Rabbi Menachem Mendel never failed to poke fun at the chasidim, especially when they boasted about the miracles performed by their rebbes. He used to say, "Only fools believe in miracles. However, the ones who do not believe that rabbis possess the capacity of performing miracles are unbelievers."

And so the turbulent soul of Rabbi Menachem Mendel dictated, and in truth his soul was restless. There was the time when a very large crowd came to Kotzk to see him. The masses struggled to enter the open doorway to shake the hand of the rabbi, or at least to see the light of his face.

After hours of waiting, a door suddenly opened and Rabbi Menachem Mendel appeared. He looked about him, saw the immense crowd of people, and sighed. Then he called to his side his disciple and son-in-law, Rabbi Abraham of Sochatzev, and in a sad and hushed voice told him: "Look at this vast crowd that stands and knocks at my door. When I was young, none of these dared to come close to me. I drove them away, I would have no part of them. Now that I am old, look at what has happened to me! Take heed, and see to it that you are more successful than I."

Rabbi Menachem Mendel was filled with great sorrow and melancholy. Often he would speak out and say: "What is the difference between me and my Rabbi Simcha Bunim of Peshischa? Rabbi Bunim always helped all who came before him; he raised them to higher levels of Jewish comprehension. I am not like that. I cannot do that, for I want everyone who comes before me to work towards his own improvement, to reach higher levels not through me, but rather by his own efforts."

In his analysis of death, Rabbi Menachem Mendel used to say: "I am not afraid of death; death does not matter at all to me. It is like a man who passes from room to room and selects the nicest one of them all."

The doors to Rabbi Menachem Mendel's house were always open. People came in and went out, and no one minded them. Disciples, chasidim — old and young moved about and around the house constantly.

When Rabbi Isaac Meir of Ger came to visit the Kotzker for the first time, he saw that there was not a segment of order in the house; he was further shocked to hear that even household utensils were stolen. While he was there he overheard the rabbi's wife and Feivel, the housekeeper, who reproachingly said, "Everything here is open, why shouldn't they steal?"

From another room Rabbi Menachem Mendel's voice was heard: "Feivel, isn't it written, *Thou shalt not steal?*"

Years later, when Rabbi Isaac Meir told this story to his chasidim, he commented, "At that moment it seemed utterly impossible for somebody to steal."

And so many, many interesting happenings have been told. A disciple once complained to Rabbi Menachem Mendel that his daughter passed away, and that he did not know why he was stricken by such a misfortune. Rabbi Menachem Mendel then asked him to explain a difficult Talmudic passage.

The disciple rubbed his forehead and explained the difficult Talmudic question. Rabbi Menachem Mendel then said, "If that is so, then you are contradicting the Tosafoth commentary."

The disciple again tried hard to explain the difficulty. Rabbi Menachem Mendel put up before the disciple progressively more difficult problems and the disciple worked very hard to reconcile all the contradictions. At the end Rabbi Menachem Mendel said, "You see that all questions have an answer, and I am sure the question that you put to God has an answer too."

The disciple regained his peace of mind and left the rabbi's room in a better spirit.

His Extremism

Rabbi Menachem Mendel was an extremist in his life's ambition to exalt the human soul — to purify, cleanse, and fortify it against the mundane, constantly oppressive problems of life. He used to say: "There are chasidim in my house of study who have the courage of pointing with their finger towards heaven and saying: 'This is my God and I shall adore Him'"(Exodus 15:2).

He was quoted as saying many times to his close followers: "I am looking for three hundred young men who would be satisfied with cabbage leaves for a head covering, who will be willing to announce from the top of the roofs: 'The Lord is God'" (I Kings 18:39).

He said: "Whenever you walk on a new road, you can be certain that nobody has spoiled it as yet."

Each saying had deep significance, such as: "To fulfill an obligation? Not at all! Either everything or nothing."

"A complete gentile is better than a half Jew," was another popular expression.

He never hesitated to say: "In no way would I choose for myself a God whose ways are intelligible to everyone born of a woman."

Another of Rabbi Menachem Mendel's sayings was: Whoever

studies the Torah and does not wear himself out; whoever sins and forgives himself; whoever prays today because he prayed yesterday — a totally wicked man is better than he."

Upon reading the passage in Genesis 43:20 — "We came indeed down at the first time to buy food" — the Rabbi of Kotzk remarked: "Did you see why we went down? To obtain food, to make a living! Is food that important that we should shame ourselves for its sake?"

Rabbi Menachem Mendel said: "Pharaoh truly had character. A man of our generation, when afflicted even with one plague, would bow to God's will and shout: 'The Rock, His work is perfect, for all His ways are justice'(Deuteronomy 32:4). However, Pharaoh had character; he accepted the ten plagues but did not change his mind."

The Rabbi of Kotzk once declared: "King Solomon said, 'For in much wisdom is much vexation' (Ecclesiastes 1:18). And so what? It is worthwhile for a man to suffer vexation as long as he continues to acquire wisdom."

Rabbi Menachem Mendel was the master of the aphorism. It is therefore worthwhile to review some of them to give us a picture of their creator.

" 'Take heed that you do not ascend the mountain or touch its fringes' (Exodus 19:12). If one does go up, he will not be satisfied by touching the fringes, but will want to ascend to the top."

" 'And they shall take for me an offering' (Ibid., 25:2). The Almighty requests of man, "Take me in a different way."

There are three festivals (*regalim*) — "As the foot (*regel*) is the basis of man, so are the holidays the basis of the weekday."

" 'Red completely' (Numbers 19:2). Red is written before completely. Red is the color and completeness the essence. If the color is within the essence, then the color becomes essence."

" 'And Abel, he also brought' (Genesis 4:4). Abel brought himself as a sacrifice."

" 'Hearken the heavens' (Deuteronomy 32:1). Hearken in a heavenly manner."

"If I am myself it is because I am myself; if you are yourself it is because you are yourself. I am therefore myself and you are yourself. But if I am myself because you are yourself, then I am not myself and you are not yourself."

"Man must be totally absorbed in the thing he is doing at a particular time."

Ethical Teachings

Rabbi Menachem Mendel, a great believer in and teacher of truth, used to say, "Everything in the world can be imitated and made to appear like the real product — all but the truth, because the truth that has been labeled falsely is not truth any longer."

It happened once that one of the very rich chasidim came to visit Rabbi Menachem Mendel. On the next day the rich man received a message that a fire had destroyed all his warehouses and that all his supplies were gone. The man became sick and fainted, his soul almost leaving him.

When Rabbi Menachem Mendel saw all this, he told him: "Quiet down. Your warehouses are not burned. Send home a telegram and you will find out that I am right."

The rich man followed the rabbi's advice. A few hours later a telegram arrived, informing him that the fire had destroyed a neighbor's warehouses and that his were left intact.

This story soon spread among the chasidim and they boasted: "Our rabbi performs miracles. He is possessed by the Holy Spirit."

"No," said Rabbi Menachem Mendel. "There are no miracles here and no Holy Spirit. It's just plain reasoning. When God Almighty inflicts punishment on a man, He chooses the punishment the afflicted can withstand. But here I saw a man completely breaking down, and I thought it impossible that God would have done it."

"And ye shall be men of holiness unto Me" (Exodus 22:30). Rabbi Menachem Mendel used to say: "This means that your holiness should be a human kind of holiness, and your human deeds should be holy. This is the quality of holiness that was requested of men. The Holy One Blessed Be He has no lack of angels. He wants holy men who are humanly holy."

Chasidim once mentioned before Rabbi Menachem Mendel that a certain chasidic rebbe was capable of seeing with his eye the seven heavenly visitors at his booth (*sukka*) on Sukkoth. To this Rabbi Menachem Mendel replied, "My vision is much clearer. They see, I believe. Belief is on a higher level than vision."

"And when she saw the ark among the reeds, she sent her handmaiden, and she took it" (Exodus 2:5). Rashi explains that Pharaoh's daughter had stretched out her hand and "Her hand increased in length many cubits, in order that she might more easily reach the cradle." Rabbi Menachem Mendel expounded, "How could Pharaoh's daughter stretch out her hand? She certainly was removed far away from Moses' basket." Immediately he replied: "From this act of Pharaoh's daughter you can learn that if a man desires something wholeheartedly he should not pay attention to the obstacles that block his road. The man should work wholeheartedly for the achievement of his purpose. He should stretch out his hand, and at the end his hand will lengthen until he achieves what he had set out to achieve."

Rabbi Menachem expounded: " 'Behold, I send a messenger before thee, to keep thee in the way and to bring thee into the place that I have prepared' (Exodus 23:20.) The emphasis is put on the words 'that I have prepared.' The character of the place, the quality of the land of Israel, these depend upon the measure of your preparation."

A young man once came to visit Rabbi Menachem Mendel. The rabbi asked him: "Where do you stand now in the study of Torah?"

To this the young man replied: "Rabbi, I have already completed all the volumes of the Talmud."

"Is that so?" answered Rabbi Menachem Mendel in amazement. "And what does the entire Talmud teach you?"

Rabbi Menachem Mendel used to say: "Pride cripples a haughty man; even if humbled by God, he always remains with his pride."

Another statement by Rabbi Menachem Mendel: "Even a completely righteous man, who never committed any sin, must be pitied. He certainly prides himself in that he never sinned, and pride is the most severe of all transgressions."

Rabbi Menachem Mendel was a man of statements such as: "All ethical qualities are an outgrowth of man's intentional strivings. The quality of humbleness is the only exception to this rule. Humbleness that is a result of intentional design should not be called humbleness any longer."

"To listen agreeably to the foolish talk of a fool," Rabbi Menachem Mendel would say, "is also a deed of charity."[11]

"And let them make Me a sanctuary, that I may dwell in the midst of them" (Exodus 25:5). This verse Rabbi Menachem Mendel explained: "That every man should build in his heart a sanctuary, so that God may dwell in it."[1]

Said the Kotzker Rabbi: "The verse in Psalms (81:8), 'I answered thee in the secret place of thunder; I proved thee at the water of *Meribah* (quarrelsomeness),' teaches us that the Lord will answer the prayer of the man who keeps his anger secret, though highly provoked by the other man's quarrelsomeness."[2]

The Kotzker Rabbi said to a usurer: "In Leviticus (25:37) we read: 'Thy money shalt thou not give him upon interest' (*beneshech*, lit., for biting). This means that you should not make your money earn the food you eat, and the borrower should work for you. Earn your living by the work of your own hands."[3]

Said the Kotzker: Three characters can be found in a man about to perform a good deed. If he says: "I shall do it soon," his character is poor. If he says: "I am ready to do it now," his character is average in quality. If he says: "I am doing it," his character is praiseworthy.[4]

A young chasid complained to the Kotzker Rabbi that many chasidim regarded the former with contempt as a "pietist." Rabbi Menachem Mendel responded, "The reason they feel contempt for one who openly exhibits his piety is that the pious man usually changes the proper places of important and unimportant things in religious conduct."[5]

A village dealer accustomed to visiting the Kotzker Rabbi frequently suddenly ceased to come. An acquaintance, who met him on the street, informed him that the rabbi had inquired about him. The dealer replied that he would come next week. When he came, the rabbi welcomed him and asked the reason for his absence. The dealer replied that he had been ashamed to visit Rabbi Menachem Mendel because he had begun to deal in adulterated honey, selling it to the purchasers as pure.

The rabbi said, "I cannot stop you in this deception at one stroke, inasmuch as you need your business for a livelihood, but I will help you out of the situation. Promise me that when you are able to secure only six cents of profit on the pound you will not handle the honey, but for seven cents you will make the transaction."

The dealer promised to do so. The next time he came, the rabbi exacted a promise not to handle the false honey under ten cents profit per pound. This was increased from time to time. To be able to sell his goods at higher prices, the dealer was compelled to offer purer honey. His customers found that the higher the price they paid the finer the honey; and they proved themselves willing to pay. Gaining the confidence of his customers, he soon acquired a monopoly of pure honey and became prosperous. The dealer heartily thanked Rabbi Menachem Mendel for showing him the pathway to integrity, and for demonstrating the truth of the axiom "Honesty is the best policy."[6]

Said Rabbi Menachem Mendel of Kotzk: "Do not hate the Jew who has wronged you; he has offended you through evil elements within him. But it may be that his good elements are greater than the goodness within yourself."[7]

A man asked the Kotzker Rabbi to pray for him in order that his sons might study Torah diligently. The rabbi replied: "If your sons will see that you are a diligent student, they will imitate you; but if you neglect your own studies and merely desire that your sons study, the result will be that they will do likewise when they grow up. They will neglect the Torah themselves and desire that their sons do the studying."[8]

A rabbi who disliked Rabbi Menachem Mendel asked him to name the greatest tzaddik alive. The Kotzker answered: "If the person you surmise may be the great tzaddik is like a spider in your eye, how much sharper will be your dislike for the person you are sure is the greatest tzaddik."⁹

Said the Kotzker: "All mitzvoth should be performed with the proper intention. There is one exception: humility."¹⁰

Rabbi Menachem Mendel told the following story: "An old man, who had long ago become an apostate, was riding on the highway one stormy night. It chanced to be the eve of Yom Kippur. The rain poured down in torrents, and the old man went under his wagon for protection. To while away the time, he began to sing, and among the songs he chanted was the melody of *Kol Nidrei.* Suddenly he recalled that it was *Kol Nidrei* night. An intense yearning overtook him to be once more with his former brethren. He left the horse and wagon and ran in the downpour towards the nearest town. At about midnight he reached the synagogue. He pushed the door open and saw that the synagogue was empty. He realized it was too late for the services, and in grief he fell to the floor. There he died soon after of a broken heart.

"Thus we see," continued the Kotzker, "that as long as there is a spark of life in a Jew we must not despair of his soul, no matter how low he may have sunk."¹¹

An ignorant villager, having heard of the mitzvah to eat and drink on the day before Yom Kippur, drank himself into a stupor. He awoke late at night, too late for *Kol Nidrei* services. Not knowing the prayers by heart, he devised a plan. He repeated the letters of the alphabet over and over, beseeching the Almighty to arrange them into the appropriate words of the prayers.

The following day he attended the Kotzker synagogue. After *Neilah* (the closing service on Yom Kippur), Rabbi Menachem Mendel summoned him to determine the cause of his absence at

Kol Nidrei. The villager confessed his transgression and asked whether his manner of reciting the prayers could be pardoned. The rabbi responded: "Your prayer was more acceptable than mine, because you uttered it with the entire devotion of your heart."[12]

There lived in Kotzk a water carrier who, though illiterate, possessed deep religious feeling. Once in shul he heard the word *tamei* (unclean), and it remained fixed in his memory. Unable to remember the customary prayers, he used the word *tamei* as his prayer, repeating it with great vehemence hundreds of times. He became the butt of the townspeople's jests and was nicknamed "Tamei." The pious water carrier ignored his mockers and continued to pour out his heart to the Creator in his own fashion.

It happened that the Kotzker Rabbi overheard his prayer. He knew it would be impossible to teach the untutored laborer the correct prayers, but wished him at least to substitute the word *tahor* (clean) for *tamei* (unclean). The water carrier repeated *tahor* many times, but soon became confused and said *tamor.* He became aware that it was unlike either the first or the second word. He ran to the rabbi tearfully and begged to be allowed his "own" word, inasmuch as he could not pray with the "rabbi's word." The Kotzker complied with his request. To this day, the water carrier was heard ardently praying: "Tamei, tamei, tamei."[13]

A man asked the Kotzker's advice regarding the wisdom of moving from his native town in order to improve his circumstances. The rabbi answered with the following story: "A certain Jew of Cracow dreamed several times that there was a treasure near a mill awaiting his arrival to dig it up. He left his house early in the morning and dug carefully, but did not find the money. The miller asked the reason for digging near his mill, and when the explanation had been given, he exclaimed: 'Why, I dreamed that there is a treasure in the courtyard of a certain man in Cracow,' and he named the digger himself. This man promptly returned to his home, and uncovered the treasure in his own yard.

"You see now," asserted the rabbi, "sometimes a man can find a treasure in his own home."[14]

The Kotzker Rabbi said: "The battle in a man's heart against evil impulses may be likened to warfare. Strategy must be employed in the inner battle exactly as in war. When the general succeeds in entrenching his position against the foe at one place, he does not rest, content with his achievement, lest the enemy assail him elsewhere. Likewise, if a man immunizes himself against a particular fault, he must guard himself against succumbing to another."[15]

Rabbi Menachem Mendel said: "There are three things desirable for success. The first: to be well born; the second: to be a good worker; the third: to have the aid of Heaven."[16]

Said the Kotzker: "The Lord brings the proud low, but the man of pride remains haughty even in his lower state; once more the Lord lowers him, and this continues until he is humbled to the very earth. On the other hand, the Lord lifts up the lowly, and he remains lowly of spirit even in his higher state. Again he is lifted up, until he attains the highest station. For this reason we say in the Chasidic prayer book: 'Who bringeth low to the ground the haughty, and raiseth up to the peak the lowly.' "[17]

The Kotzker Rabbi said that joyfulness is the outcome of holiness. Therefore, Sukkoth, coming after Yom Kippur, when we become holy and sinless, is called the "season of our joy."[18]

A widow was sued for rent before the Sochatzover Rabbi. She

began to weep copiously. The rabbi refused to hear the case, on the grounds that he had learned from the Kotzker that tears were a form of bribery, and that he might henceforth be biased in her favor.[19]

Rabbi Menachem Mendel's aphorisms were quite varied. He was heard to declare: " 'With happiness you shall depart' (Isaiah 55:12). With happiness you can depart from your troubles."[20]

Torah

Once Rabbi Menachem Mendel entered the house of study and saw two of his most learned disciples arguing vehemently about the meaning of a certain Talmudic passage.

The rabbi listened attentively to their arguments and then remarked: "If you look up the Corrections of the thief of Wilno, you will find that you have no argument."

All eyes turned toward Rabbi Menachem Mendel. How could such a holy person speak so disrespectfully about His Eminence, Rabbi Elijah of Wilno?

Rabbi Menachem Mendel then explained: "All of us know that Moses received the Torah at Sinai with all its secrets and most intricate explanations. Moses knew everything that any future Jewish scholar might find in the Torah. However, some souls present at Mount Sinai were hidden behind Moses' back, and listened to all the secrets and involved explanations. Among them was Rabbi Elijah of Wilno. In his Corrections, he illustrates with one stroke of his pen the most involved problems. What a fine thief the Gaon of Wilno was."

The Kotzker said: "We are told in the Midrash that Korach asked Moses: 'Is a house filled with Torah scrolls free from the obligation to have a *mezuzah* nailed to the doorpost?' The answer was in the negative. This question may be explained allegorically thus: 'Is a scholar, who understands the reasons for the precepts of the Law, free from the obligation to actually perform them?' The answer is that he is not free, but he must observe them in practice."

The Kotzker Rabbi gave two reasons for our naming the Feast of Shavuoth "the time of the giving of our Torah," and not "the time of our receiving the Torah." One reason was that while the Torah was given to us only in the time of Moses we continue to receive the Torah throughout history as well. The second reason was that while the Torah was given to every Jew alike it was not received by everyone in equal proportion, since the receiving depends upon the power of understanding in each individual.

Once, in a year of drought, the price of food had risen extensively and there was general suffering. Several chasidim who visited the Kotzker Rabbi on the Sabbath wished to receive his farewell blessing and leave for their homes, but the rabbi refused them permission to depart. The rabbi's wife inquired as to why he was holding them over at a time when inn prices were prohibitive.

The rabbi replied: "The reason food is expensive and learning is cheap is because everyone demands food, but few are anxious to learn. Let people care more for study and less for food, and you will perceive that food will be cheap and learning expensive."

Said the Kotzker: "The Sages teach us that we should not believe the man who professes to have labored hard in the study of the Torah and finds himself unable to comprehend it. How do the Sages come to make this statement? — from the Torah, which states that God's words are not in heaven but are near to man. Hence, since every Jew is near to the Torah, it follows that if he makes a sincere effort to understand it, he must attain his wish —

else it would be as if the Torah were in heaven, at least for this man.

"It is like one who has lost a diamond in a stack of hay. He does not abandon his efforts to find it, no matter now long it requires, for he is sure the diamond is there. Likewise, the Torah assures you that the Word of God is near to you, and is within your comprehension. Do not abandon your effort, for you will surely discover eventually that you understand it."

Unconventionality

It was told that a young man came immediately after his wedding to the Rabbi of Kotzk, in tears. The rabbi asked him: "Why are you crying?"

The young man sobbed, "I married a woman and my father-in-law did not give me a prayer shawl (*talith*)."

The rabbi answered, "You can wrap yourself in the four fringes of the earth."

Once Rabbi Menachem Mendel visited the town of Guryea, where he was born and raised. Among the first people whom he visited was his elementary school teacher, who had taught him the rudiments of reading. Close by lived his Talmud teacher, whom the rabbi did not honor with a visit.

The peeved Talmud teacher came to his illustrious pupil and inquired: "Why did you not come and pay your respects to me? Did I not teach you more than your elementary school teacher?"

"I surely agree with you," replied the rabbi. "You taught me much more. You taught me many things about which I am not certain and about the meaning of which I am not completely sure. This one explains it in such a way, and then comes along somebody else and questions it and explains it differently.

However, my first teacher, who taught me the ABC's — his teachings are unquestionable. Everybody must admit that an A is an A and a B is a B."

He also said: "The freedom of man is more important than the study of Torah. Every man should strain his mind to the utmost and get the complete meaning of the chapter in Exodus which relates how the Jews gained their freedom. This is more important than any problem in the Tosafoth commentary."

On the Aggadic statement: "In the same way as the outward appearances of people differ, so do their opinions" (Bemidbar Rabba 21), Rabbi Menachem Mendel explained: "In the same way that you tolerate people whose appearance is different than your own, so must you tolerate the opinions of others, even if they are not in agreement with your own views and convictions."

Near Kotzk there is a forest where Rabbi Menachem Mendel used to walk frequently. One day his intimates accompanied him on a walk there. Suddenly they came upon a beautiful tree. The Kotzker Rabbi turned to his chasidim and said: "You must certainly remember the following Mishna: 'He who is walking on the road studying, and stops his studies and declares, "How beautiful is this tree; how beautiful is this plant" — the Torah considers him to be deserving of death.' It is difficult to understand this, for the tree is one of God's first creations; why shouldn't we express our admiration of this glory and praise the greatness of the Creator in this creation?"

The rabbi then grew silent and his chasidim were quiet as well. The air was warm and heavy, the sun scorching hot. Thus the day was spent, until darkness began to fall. Towards evening, the heavens became heavy with clouds. One of the chasidim remarked, "We had better travel home before it rains."

Meanwhile, it became very dark; one man could not see the other. Soon heavy rains began to fall, accompanied by thunder and lightning.

Suddenly a man's cries were heard from the distance. Everyone became silent. The rabbi rose and told the teamster to go and see who was screaming. The frightened teamster moved quickly. When he returned, he told of two thunder-stricken gentiles lying on the road, crying for help. The chasidim hurried to them, loaded them into the wagon, and brought them to the city.

Meanwhile, the rain had stopped. The moon came out, illuminating the road. The rabbi said, "Let us go home. The first chapter of loving Israel we have carried out under a beautiful tree with two gentiles — this is the purpose of the author of the Mishna: 'He who is walking in the road and stops his studies is deserving of death.' If it rains, everybody wants to hurry home and stop his studies. But it is forbidden to do this, because you might be endangering human lives. Two gentiles might have died. But because we did not stop our studies and paid no attention to the rain, we were privileged to carry out the commandment of saving lives."

The chasid who related the story concluded by describing how, during the walk, the rabbi had talked repeatedly about love of Israel. By true love of Israel, we learn to love the whole world.[1]

Chapter 10 — Notes

Ethical Teachings points 1-20 have been translated by Lewis I. Newman in his book *The Hasidic Anthology,* N.Y., 1944.

Ethical Teachings
 1. Newman, p. 8, #6
 2. Newman, p. 26, #4
 3. Newman, p. 29, #2
 4. Newman, p. 318, #2
 5. Newman, p. 77, #4
 6. Newman, p. 87, #1
 7. Newman, p. 118, #3
 8. Newman, p. 93, #5
 9. Newman, p. 191, #25
10. Newman, p. 211, #5
11. Newman, p. 212, #7
12. Newman, p. 499, #1
13. Newman, p. 275, #4
14. Newman, p. 432, #7
15. Newman, p. 285, #1
16. Newman, p. 355, #17
17. Newman, p. 464, #1
18. Newman, p. 508, #2
19. Fox, p. 87, D
20. Fox, p. 87, F

Unconventionality
 1. Fox, pp. 84-85

Chapter 11

Disciples

The Rabbi of Kotzk was a true heir of Israel Ba'al Shem Tov, the great teacher of men and molder of character. Among Rabbi Menachem Mendel's disciples were many of the greatest sons of contemporary Polish Jewry — men who by leadership and learning became the recognized leaders of their generation. Kotzk served as a preparatory school for many of the chasidic greats, who became recognized rabbis and famous leaders of the movement after the passing of Rabbi Menachem Mendel. Some achieved this distinction during his lifetime as well.

Many of the most capable young men were attracted to the fame of Kotzk, where they spent weeks and months under the tutelage of their rabbi. Here their character took shape, their outlook on life crystallized, and their learning deepened. Under the impact of Rabbi Menachem Mendel's personality and teaching, they achieved their spiritual and intellectual maturity, and in their later life they continued to carry out the mission for which they had been prepared.

The most distinguished of the Kotzker chasidim was Rabbi Isaac Meir. His status was that of a junior colleague, and had he desired it, he could have been proclaimed "rabbi" by his manifold admirers immediately after the passing of Rabbi Simcha Bunim.

However, he preferred to step aside to allow Rabbi Menachem Mendel to occupy the seat of leadership. Later he explained his faithfulness to Rabbi Menachem Mendel in the following way. "I saw a large bolt of fire and I bent myself under it for twenty-six years."

On a different occasion, when asked why he traveled to Kotzk when he could be a rabbi in his own right, he answered: "Scripture teaches us: 'Buy the truth and sell it not' (Proverbs 23:23). As long as I can buy the truth, there is no need for me to sell."

He remained loyal to his rabbi under all circumstances, and always found a sound justification for the latter's actions. When the dissatisfied chasidim complained to him about their rabbi's severity and proneness to anger, he explained to them: "In this respect our rabbi is like our forefather Jacob. Of all the three Patriarchs we hear that only Jacob was really capable of becoming angry — 'And Jacob's anger was kindled against Rachel' (Genesis 30:2). Jacob knew how to get angry, and so does our rabbi. . . . It is true that the Talmud prohibits us from applying undue pressures and obligations if they are not for the sake of Heaven; however, whatever our rabbi does is for the sake of Heaven."

Once Rabbi Isaac Meir brought to Kotzk a manuscript of his own which he had labored on many years: a commentary on Choshen Mishpat, one of the sections of the Shulchan Aruch. Before publishing it he wanted his rabbi's opinion. Rabbi Menachem Mendel read through the manuscript carefully and praised Rabbi Isaac Meir's soundness of judgment and conclusions.

During the conversation, the Kotzker remarked that this commentary, when published, would replace the work of

158

Shabbatai Cohen (Shach), and that perhaps it wasn't right for a book of a contemporary writer to overshadow an accepted classic in Jewish law. Rabbi Isaac Meir then ran home quickly, built a fire, and threw in the manuscript. While doing so, he pronounced loudly the benediction: "Blessed be Thou, our God, who hast commanded us to hearken to the words of the Sages."

A short time after the death of Rabbi Isaac Meir's brother, a friend of the deceased came and told how in a dream the departed had complained that he had no rest in the hereafter because this friend had not kept the proper time for prayer. Rabbi Isaac Meir advised the friend to tell the deceased that he followed the ways of the Kotzker Rabbi and that the deviation was, therefore, approved by sufficient authority.

Once, during a very severe spell of winter weather, Rabbi Isaac Meir brought his two young grandchildren to Kotzk. When asked why he exposed the children to such an inconvenience, he replied: "It is worthwhile for them to suffer so that they can see a real Jew." One of the boys, Aryeh Leib, who later became famous as the second Rabbi of Ger and author of *Sefat Emet,* never forgot this trip and prided himself on the fact that he was among the original Kotzker chasidim.[1]

Another old-timer from Peshischa who joined the ranks of Rabbi Menachem Mendel's chasidim was Rabbi Chanoch HaCohen. After the passing of Rabbi Isaac Meir, he was declared tzaddik, at the age of seventy, by many of the chasidim, and achieved fame as the Rabbi of Alexander. He was thus second in the line of succession after Rabbi Menachem Mendel. He used to explain in true chasidic fashion what had brought him to Kotzk, where mysticism and logic coexisted. Once in a dream he saw Rabbi Menachem Mendel, and behind him the departed Rabbi

Simcha Bunim. He ran to his deceased master, Rabbi Bunim, and cried: "With whom did you leave me, Rabbi?" Rabbi Bunim pointed with his finger to Rabbi Menachem Mendel.

The most eminent among the future greats who grew up under the Rabbi of Kotzk's influence was his son-in-law, Abraham Borenstein, known as the first chasidic rabbi of Sochatzev. He always referred to his father-in-law as "an angel of God," and never tired of saying that all his learning had come from Rabbi Menachem Mendel. This was quite a compliment, if we keep in mind that Rabbi Abraham was regarded by his contemporaries as one of Polish Jewry's greatest Talmudic scholars.

The chasidic biographers quote his expressions: "My teacher and father-in-law, the source of all Torah and wisdom. . . . I have met many rabbis and tzaddikim, but my father-in-law from Kotzk was an angel of God. . . . It is clear to me that even the Messiah will not bring the hearts of Israel closer to their Father in heaven than did Rabbi Menachem Mendel bring his chasidim."

After the passing of Rabbi Chanoch HaCohen of Alexander, many of the orphaned chasidim turned to Rabbi Abraham for leadership. In spite of his unwillingness to assume the role of a tzaddik (1870), he repeatedly announced: "Whosoever is not proficient in the Torah and does not engage with all his senses in its study, let him not come to me." When the number of his followers continued to grow, he used to say that he would like to be sent away to a lonely island with ten students and study there uninterruptedly. By "Torah," the Rabbi of Sochatzev meant Talmud. He argued that "Kabbala is the soul of the Torah," but students should not be too much concerned with its mysteries. The main subject of study should be the Talmud, and it should be studied in a clear, logical way. The purpose of study is spiritual refinement. "The Torah refines matter."[2]

Rabbi Yechiel Meir, famous as the Rabbi of Gostinin and the chief character in Shalom Asch's novel *Salvation,* was also a disciple of the Kotzker. He used to say that under the influence of Rabbi Menachem Mendel he completely lost all feelings of hatred toward his fellow men, because his rabbi made him love his enemy as much as he did his best friend. Once, when he returned home after Simchath Torah from a prolonged stay in Kotzk, his relatives asked him if the Torah was received any differently in Kotzk than in his hometown. When he answered them in the affirmative, they insisted that he tell them where the difference lay.

Rabbi Yechiel Meir then asked his relatives: "Tell me, how do you explain the commandment: 'Do not steal' ?"

They answered: "Do not steal from others."

He then expounded: "In Kotzk we teach that you must not steal even from yourself."

Once, on Purim, when the Kotzker was secluded in his room and refused to see even his closest chasidim, Rabbi Yechiel Meir knocked on the door and Rabbi Menachem Mendel opened it. He then told him: "Rabbi, today is Purim and we give alms to every beggar who stretches out his hand and begs for help. Rabbi, I am naked and forsaken; clothe me and take care of me."

The rabbi took him into his room and spent an entire day with him. Rabbi Yechiel Meir was one of the very few people to whom the Kotzker offered a chair. Once, when asked about the whereabouts of the anonymous thirty-six righteous men of his generation, the Kotzker Rabbi replied: "And what is our Yechiel Meir short of?"[3]

In addition to the above-mentioned main flag-bearers of post-Kotzk chasiduth in Poland, chasidic tradition kept intact the memory of a number of men who were influenced by Rabbi Menachem Mendel in their formative years. Throughout their lifetimes, their character, bearing, and demeanor served as a living reminder of the great school of character that Kotzk once was. The life stories of these men helped to perpetuate the legend of Kotzk, and the ensuing generations of chasidim saw in them sparks left over from the grand flame that once illumined the horizon of Kotzk.

One of these men was Rabbi Abraham of Porisov, a grandson of "The Holy Jew" of Peshischa. He came to Kotzk for the first time at age fourteen and was seventeen when Rabbi Menachem Mendel died. But throughout his entire life the chasidim saw in him an embodiment of the high ethical standards inculcated by his master. Truth and modesty were his guiding stars, even though he had to pay a very exacting price for maintaining these principles. To the chasidim he was a living reminder that even scions of prominent families were capable of "annihilation" of their being and of reconstruction of their personalities along the desired lines, if they seriously set out to do this.[4]

Rabbi Abraham Leib of Brok carried out in his own way the practice of humility taught in Kotzk. When he published his two volumes on Talmudic lore in 1885, he did so anonymously. He did not want to be in the limelight as the author of a book; important were the ideas he taught, but not the man who proclaimed them.

His helpfulness to others knew no bounds. Once, while Rabbi Leib was visiting the tzaddik of Ger, a petitioner came after midnight with an urgent plea and begged to be admitted at once to the tzaddik. When refused admission, he turned to Rabbi Abraham Leib for help. The aged rabbi got dressed and walked beyond the city limits in a heavy winter storm; there, outside of the legal area of jurisdiction of the Rabbi of Ger, he listened to the petitioner's supplication for help.

Rabbi Baruch of Czizev was known for his strong character and unusual will power. When he told the Rabbi of Kotzk that he had decided to leave his native town of Stuczin to become Rabbi of Czizev, Rabbi Menachem Mendel said: "The Ba'al Shem made his appearance in Podolia and thus corrected the situation which Scripture describes as 'and their fear of Me is a commandment of men learned by rote' (Isaiah 29:13). The Maggid moved to Wolyn in order to achieve the same there. Rabbi Elimelech of Lizensk did it in Galicia, and the tzaddikim of Lublin and Peshischa brought chasiduth to Poland. It is now your turn to continue with the same in Lithuania."

However, Rabbi Baruch held his own ground and replied: "Before I bring chasiduth to Lithuania, I must bring it to myself; and I am not through with myself as yet."

It was the accepted chasidic custom to consult the tzaddik before the marriage of one's children. Rabbi Baruch, however, did not comply with this and informed Rabbi Menachem Mendel about his son's wedding after it was over. "Why did you not ask my advice?" marveled the Rabbi of Kotzk.

"Because we know that in matters of matrimony you do not know more than we do," was the reply.

After the passing of Rabbi Isaac Meir of Ger (1866), Rabbi Baruch yielded to the plea of his townspeople and allowed them to proclaim him tzaddik. He soon became famous as a great miracle performer, and the poor and unfortunate flocked to his residence. Rabbi Baruch made it known to his close circle of intimates that he expected to be a guide for people desiring spiritual and moral perfection, and not simply a provider of cures and dispenser of blessings. However, he continued performing the everyday chores of a popular tzaddik, explaining: "As we have to accept the good sent by God, so do we have to accept the evil. As I am happy to help a man climb to higher levels of Torah and worship, so must I be content to listen to all the complaints and misfortunes of man."[5]

Another Lithuanian to become an ardent follower of Kotzk was Rabbi Meshl of Bialystok. As a boy he spent days and nights in the house of study, and the greatest rabbis were startled by the depth of his Talmudic knowledge. He often heard people poking fun at the chasidim and decided to learn the truth about them for himself. He went to visit the house of worship of the Kotzker chasidim in Bialystok, joined in their meditations, and was soon drawn into their circle of dancers. Later he visited Kotzk. From there he went to Lubavitch to explore the Chabad system of chasiduth, and afterwards he returned to Kotzk.

After the passing of Rabbi Menachem Mendel and Rabbi Isaac Meir, there was nothing to keep him in the diaspora, and in 1869 he moved with his entire family to Jerusalem. In Palestine he became the main exponent of the Kotzk brand of chasiduth, and his house of prayer was a central attraction for students of the Kabbala. During his lifetime he published seven volumes, dealing mostly with mysticism, and a number of his writings remained in manuscript.

Rabbi Zev Wolf was the son-in-law of one of the richest men in Strikov, and famous for his unusual strength in Talmudic learning. The Kotzker chasidim in town were tireless in their efforts to win over this studious boy, and did not rest until they succeeded in bringing him to Kotzk. The first Sabbath in Kotzk made an unusual impression on the young convert to chasiduth, and he remained a chasid his entire life. He soon gained the reputation of being second to Rabbi Isaac Meir in Talmudic learning and first in Kotzk in sharp wit and quick mind.

His wisdom was admired by everybody. It was customary in Kotzk for a certain rich chasid to present the rabbi with a gift of an *ethrog* on every Sukkoth eve. After a number of years this man lost his wealth and brought to his rabbi an *ethrog* of lesser quality. Another chasid, who aspired the privilege of having the rabbi pronounce the blessings over an *ethrog* brought by him, supplied him with one of unusual beauty.

Rabbi Menachem Mendel called in his disciples, and asked them to decide which of the two was the nicer *ethrog*. The chasidim were captivated by the unusual appearance of the one brought by the second man. The master then called in Rabbi Zev Wolf and asked him for his opinion. Rabbi Zev at once proclaimed the first *ethrog* to be of higher value, and Rabbi Menachem Mendel accepted his opinion. Rabbi Zev Wolf was also unique among the Kotzker chasidim for his skill in composing Hebrew epigrams and satires.

Rabbi Zelig of Shranzk enjoyed the reputation of being the oldest man among the chasidim who came to Kotzk. During his lifetime he visited sixty tzaddikim, until he was finally attracted to the Rabbi of Kotzk, and remained a faithful follower to his last day. Once, Rabbi Menachem Mendel told him that he should stay home and not expose himself to the hardships of travel. To this Rabbi Zelig replied: "My home is the rabbi's house of study."

Rabbi Moses Michal of Biala was attracted to chasiduth at an early age, but he did not make any pilgrimages to a tzaddik's court until one year after his father's demise. This was his way of observing the commandment to "Honor thy father." In Peshischa he met Rabbi Menachem Mendel and the two became friends. A man of considerable financial means, he provided Rabbi Menachem Mendel and his family for years with their material needs.

According to chasidic tradition, the Rabbi of Kotzk once told him to stop supporting him. When pressed for a reason, he explained: "When God wants to test a man through poverty, He takes away his means of earning a livelihood. And why should you become poor on my behalf?"

However, Rabbi Moses Michal insisted that he would continue to do the same. He soon lost all his possessions, and was invited to take over the seat of Rabbi of Biala through the help of the Rabbi of Kotzk. He became famous for his extreme adherence to truth and justice, and for not allowing any exterior considerations to interfere with his strivings for perfection on the personal and community levels.

Rabbi Pinchas Elijah (Pinye) of Pilch was considered an individualist *sui generis* among the Kotzker chasidim. Kotzk disliked rapturous prayer. The heart should not be put in a state of ecstasy through the means of violent hand and body movements. On the contrary, the blissful heart that overflows with beatitude might sometimes express itself in a swaying of the body or an excitement of a limb. Such a kind of enchantment was permissible, and the entranced prayers of Rabbi Pinchas Elijah were regarded as belonging to this category.

When he lost his inherited fortune in a bad business deal, the people of Pilch offered him the post of rabbi. He made his appointment conditional upon the following three terms: 1) the townspeople would not come to him to settle their petty business controversies; 2) he would be freed from the duty of delivering sermons; and 3) he would not be prevented from making a pilgrimage to his rabbi. In desperation, the townspeople appealed to the Rabbi of Ger, and only his intervention prompted Rabbi Pinchas Elijah to withdraw his conditions.

Rabbi Hirsch of Tomashov was one of the best known Kotzk chasidim. He and the future master met in the Tomashov house of study, and after that he became Rabbi Menachem Mendel's most faithful follower. Together with Rabbi Menachem Mendel he belonged to the inner circle of Peshischa, and when the former was proclaimed tzaddik Rabbi Hirsch assumed the duties of his household manager. No visitor could enter the study of the Rabbi of Kotzk without receiving a nod of approval from Rabbi Hirsch. His devotion to his rabbi was boundless. Himself a man of means, he did not derive any material benefits from his dedicated service. Once a year he visited every city where there was an organized group of Kotzk chasidim, and collected the annual contribution for the maintenance of the rabbi's "court." These visits were an occasion for celebration and festivities. He was regarded as the personal messenger of the rabbi and the supreme arbiter for the settlement of all affairs.

The greatest personal reward that he received for his dedication came on the day of his only daughter's wedding. The Rabbi of Kotzk was then in solitary confinement and refused to see his chasidim. However, he came out from his solitude and pronounced the benedictions at the marriage ceremony, adding the words that were later repeated for generations by the children and grandchildren of the newlywed: "She is an only daughter, a daughter of fine character, a daughter of an excellent family."

Typical was the case of Rabbi Noah of Karov. He was a

disciple of the Seer of Lublin. After the Seer's death, when thirty of his followers declared themselves to be tzaddikim, Rabbi Noah was attracted to one of them. Upon his master's death, he was declared tzaddik by the chasidim of the deceased. Rabbi Noah accepted the post of a chasidic community leader and at the same time began his annual pilgrimages to the Rabbi of Kotzk. He usually came with a retinue of his chasidim. Kotzker chasidim did not accept people who served in a dual capacity of tzaddik and chasid, but in the case of Rabbi Noah they made an exception. They recognized his sincerity and purity of purpose.

The same held true of Rabbi Samuel of Shinova. He was at the same time a devoted disciple of two tzaddikim, of Rabbi Simcha Bunim of Peshischa and of Rabbi Leib of Lentshno. He also came to Kotzk. Rabbi Menachem Mendel accepted him into his confidence and respected him highly.

Rabbi Samuel served his rabbi in one more unusual way: in his book *Ramatayim Tzofim* he mentioned the Kotzker's teachings and a few episodes from his life. Disregarding a few other data, this book and the writings of Rabbi Abraham of Sochatzev are the only first-hand documents we possess about the teachings of Rabbi Menachem Mendel of Kotzk. All the other tracts were written two generations later, by the grandchildren of the original Kotzker chasidim.

It is not necessary to mention here the names of all the disciples of the Kotzker who played a leading role in the life of Polish Jewry. To do so would bring us to the history of the Polish rabbinate and force us to go beyond the confines set for this study. Isaac Alfasi and Yehuda Leib Levin, in their monographs, follow the stories of sixty former disciples of Kotzk who achieved fame and had a part in molding the minds of their generation.

Chapter 11 — Notes

This chapter is based upon the section "Talmidov" in *Amud Ha'Emet,* pp. 10-112; chapter 10 of Alfasi, *HaRabbi Mi'Kotzk;* the two volumes of Yehuda Leib Levin, *Beth Kotzk;* and Eliezer Steinman, *Be'er HaChasidut, Sefer al Admorey Polin.*

1. *Amud Ha'Emet,* pp. 101-104
2. *Amud Ha'Emet,* pp. 104-107; *Beth Kotzk,* vol. 2, p. 55
3. Levin, *l. c.,* vol. 1, p. 118
4. Levin, *l. c.,* vol 1, p. 26
5. Levin, *l. c.,* vol. 1, pp. 60-67

Chapter 12

The Legacy of Kotzk

The life story of Rabbi Menachem Mendel, which has been reconstructed in the preceding pages, has implications reaching far beyond the confines of mere biography. Whatever was said or done in Kotzk exerted a profound influence on untold numbers of followers. He was not only a great personality but also an important factor in shaping the intellectual history of his generation.

He was of the great figures that were a living incarnation of the spirit of their era, and at the same time foreshadowed the developments of the imminent future. His mind was molded by the established and deep-rooted ideas of the past, together with the budding and still shapeless notions of the impending tomorrow. All of this made the Rabbi of Kotzk a typical representative of an era of transition; and times of transition are usually fraught with inner tensions and seemingly self-contradictory problems. This transition was the source of his greatness and also of his frustration.

The personality of Rabbi Menachem Mendel was molded by the combined impact of three currents of thought, forming the Jewish spiritual and intellectual tradition. Talmudic learning, mystical strivings, and philosophic thinking, when taken in

170

isolation, might have presented three somewhat contradictory aspects in the development of traditional Judaism. However, in the mind of the Rabbi of Kotzk, these three influences merged into one unified design for Jewish thinking and living.

The Kotzk system restored the supremacy of Torah learning among the rank and file of the Polish chasidim, and this legacy of Kotzk was faithfully preserved by the movement's subsequent leaders. The latent mystical inclinations and strivings for communion with the Divine added an intense feeling, tone, and emotional depth to the Talmudic intellectualism and ethical perfectionism propagated by Kotzk.

As a result of this development, the Zohar and the Lurian Kabbala lost their hold on the minds of almost all segments of Polish Jewry. Logical thinking and an attitude of open-mindedness to the surrounding world slowly became the dominating traits of *mithnaged* and chasid alike. Rabbi Menachem Mendel's inner world might have been dominated by mystical ideas at times, but this remained with him an individual characteristic that was not transferred to his followers. In his role as a teacher and spiritual leader, he insisted on the primacy of learning and ethical living. As in the remote Talmudic past, mysticism was again relegated to the chosen few who could be safely intrusted with its mysteries; the rank and file were discouraged from delving into its unfathomed depth.

This restoration of learning and logical thinking necessitated a different kind of chasiduth. Kotzk declared a merciless war on the chasidic leaders who won their hold on the masses through promises of intercession with the Divine for the sake of curing the sick or winning material gain. The tzaddik is not a mediator who carries the petitions of Israel to their Father in heaven, but rather a spiritual leader who has attained the highest degree of learning and exemplary Jewish living. The tzaddik thus serves as a living embodiment of the Jewish ideal of man.

The days of the chasidic rebbe should not be taken up with listening to the troubles and misfortunes of his faithful; his main preoccupations should be their spiritual uplift and day-by-day guidance in the proper ways of Jewish living. Every man should be encouraged to rely on himself in solving his life problems and should be trained to turn directly to God for help. The road to the Heavenly Throne is open to everybody, and all men are equal before the face of God. He accepts everybody's prayers when they are uttered with sincerity and devotion.

The art of prayer is one of man's greatest accomplishments. Through prayer the soul achieves union with God. Man should know how to put himself in a state of spiritual preparedness that is congenial for prayer. Only then can it become a rejuvenating and soul-stirring religious experience, during which man actually speaks to God. Prayer conceived in this manner is not a mere habitual exercise of duty, but one of the greatest attainments a chasid is capable of achieving.

This was the Kotzk synthesis between the intellectual and mystical components of traditional Judaism. Mysticism turned loose and abused became the feeding ground for mass superstition and self-delusion bordering on primitive magic. The Kotzk system curtailed the rise of the irrational, transforming it into channels that deepened man's religious emotion. This constantly renewed religiosity, together with the study and practice of Jewish precepts, gave rise to the Kotzk system of ethics and the strivings for constant self-perfection.

The glowing religious atmosphere surrounding the Rabbi of

Kotzk exerted an unusual soul-shaping influence on the chasidim and stamped them with specific character traits. This was probably the reason why in Jewish folklore and literature the expression "an old Kotzker chasid" was synonymous with an unusually great Jewish personality.

This peculiar fusion of the rational and non-rational properties of Jewish tradition created the Kotzk system of chasiduth, and made Rabbi Menachem Mendel the grand standard bearer of Jewish religious revival. This was the legacy of Kotzk.

BIBLIOGRAPHY

Sources

Amud Ha'Emet, Tel Aviv (no year of publication given)

Bergman, Eliezer: *Kotzker Mayses*, Warsaw 1924

Borenstein, Abraham: *Avney Nezer*

Borenstein, Abraham: *Egley Tal*, Peterkov 1905

Buber, Martin: *Or HaGanuz*, Tel Aviv 1940

Buber, Martin: *Tales of the Hasidim, The Early Masters*, New York 1947

Buber, Martin: *Tales of the Hasidim, The Later Masters*, New York 1948

Gliksman, Pinchas Zelig, *Tiferet Adam*, Lodz 1933

HaCohen, Chanoch Henoch: *Chashava LeTovah*, Protrkow 1929

Kadish, I. K.: *Siach Sarfey Kodesh*, Lodz 1888

Leshon Chasidim, Lvov 1876 (no author indicated)

Mamlak, Zvi Yehuda: *Abir HaRoim*, Peterkov 1938

Marcus, Aaron: *HaChasidut* (translated from the German), Tel Aviv 1954

Mordechai Motel ben Zev Wolf of Strikov: *Doresh Tov*, Warsaw 1900

Moshe, Jerachmiel: *Niflaot Chadashot*, Peterkov 1896

Moshe Yechiel, of Jadimow: *Likutim Chadashim*, Warsaw 1899

Newman, Louis I.: *Hasidic Anthology*, New York 1944

Ohel Torah, Lublin 1909

Ortn, Israel Jacob: *Emet V'Emuna*, Jerusalem 1940

Walden, Aaron: *Shem HaGedolim HeChadash*, Warsaw 1864

Werfel, Yitzchak: *Sefer HaChasidut*, Tel Aviv 1945

Yeushsohn, I.: *Fun Alten Ojtzer*, Warsaw 1932

Yosfa, Elijah bar Abraham: *Eyzor Eliyahu*, Warsaw 1885

Zev of Strikow, *Zer Zahav Keter Torah*, Warsaw 1900

Zvi, Moshe: *Meir Eyney Hagola*, Peterkov 1928

Monographs

Alfasi, Yitzchak: *Ha'Rabbi Mi'Kotzk*, Tel Aviv 1952

Arigur, I.: *Kotzk*, Tel Aviv 1935

Ascoli, Aaron Zev: "HaChasidut b'Polin," in *Beth Israel b'Polin*, vol. 2, Jerusalem 1944 (Israel Heilperin, editor)

Biletsky, Israel C.: *Beim Kvartel von Kotsk*, Israel-Buch, Tel Aviv 1975

Buber, Martin: *Hasidism and Modern Man*, New York 1958

Buber, Martin: *Ten Rungs: Hasidic Sayings*, New York 1947

Byk, Abraham: *Welt un Haym*, New York 1941

Byk, Abraham: *Hassides Motiven*, New York 1944

Byk, Abraham: "Yesod Ha'Omanut BaChasidut," *Hadoar*, 4 Tamuz 5705 (1945)

Dinaburg, Benzion: "Reshita shel HaChasidut V'Yesodoteha HaSozialiim

V'HaMeshichiim," *Zion*, vol. 8 (1934), vol. 9 (1935), vol. 10 (1945)

Dubnow, Simon: *Toldot HaChasidut* (2 vol.), Tel Aviv 1930-32

Dubnow, Simon: *History of the Jews in Russia and Poland* (2 vol.), Philadelphia 1916

Edelbaum, M.: "Toldot HaChasidut B'Polariva," *Ha'Olam,* Shvat 5687 (Jan. 1927), London

Eibeshutz, Yochanan Levi: *Simcha Bunim of Peshischa,* Tel Aviv 1965

Elzet, Yehuda: "Kotzk," *Mizrachi,* 1920, No. 67, Warsaw

Erlich, Israel: *Rabbi Mendele Mi'Kotzk,* Tel Aviv 1952

Feinkind, Moshe: *Gute Yiden in Poilen,* Warsaw 1936

Finkel, Joshua: "A Psychoanalytic Prefiguration in Hasidic Literature," *Eidenu,* New York, 1942

Finkel, Joshua: *Menahem Morgenstern of Kotzk, in Jewish Leaders,* Leo Jung, editor, New York 1953

Finkelstein, Leo: *Megillat Polin,* Buenos Aires 1947

Geshuri, M. S.: "L'Korot Ha'Vigun HaChasidi," *Sefer Azkara L'Harav Kook,* Jerusalem 1949

Geshuri, M. S.: "Negina U'Menagnim B'Kotzk" in *Heychal Kotzk*

Gliksman, Pinchas Zelig: *Der Kotzker Rebbe* (2 vol.), Peterkov 1938; a Hebrew translation is to be found in *Heychal Kotzk,* Rothenberg and Shenfeld, editors, Tel Aviv 1959

Graubart, Yehuda Leib: "V'Hitzdikku et HaTzaddik," *Mizrachi,* 1920, No. 67, Warsaw

Heschel, Abraham J.: "The Inner World of The Polish Jew," *Polish Jews, A Pictorial Record,* by Roman Vishniac, New York 1947

Heschel, Abraham J.: *A Passion for Truth,* New York 1973

Heschel, Abraham J.: "Rabbi Mendel Mi'Kotzk," *Hadoar,* 28 Iyar 5719, New York

Horodezky, S. A.: *HaChasidut VeHaChasidim* (4 vol.), 4th edition, Tel Aviv 1953

Levin, Yehuda Leib: *Bet Kotzk* (3 vol.), Jerusalem 1959

Minkin, Jacob S.: *The Romance of Hasidism,* New York 1935

Prager, Moshe: "Mi'Kotzk v'ad Gur," in *Hadoar 25 Shvat 5719, New York*

Rabinowitz, Zvi Meir: *Rabbi Yaakov Yitzchak Mi'Peshischa,* Peterkov 1932

Rabinovitz, Zvi Meir: *Rabbi Simcha Bunim Mi'Peshischa,* Tel Aviv 1945

Rothenberg, Yechezkel & Shenfeld, Moshe (editors): *Heychal Kotzk,* Tel Aviv 1959

Schechter, Solomon: *The Chasidim,* Studies in Judaism, vol. 1, Philadelphia 1945

Schwartzman, Meyer: *Der Yiddisher Flam,* Winnipeg 1958

Scholem, Gershom G.: *Major Trends in Jewish Mysticism,* New York 1941

Shemen, Nachman: *Lublin,* Toronto 1951

Steinman, Eliezer: *Be'er HaChasidut, Admorey Polin,* Tel Aviv (no date of publication given)
Steinman, Eliezer: *Be'er HaChasidut, HaSava Mi'Shpala,* Tel Aviv (no date)
Steinman, Eliezer: *Sha'ar HaChasidut,* Tel Aviv 1957
Unger, Menashe: *Hasides un Leben,* New York 1946
Urian, Meir: *Sne Boer b'Kotzk,* Jerusalem 1961
Waxman, Meyer, *A History of Jewish Literature,* vol. 3, New York 1936
Weinryb, Shlomo, "Kotzker Hasides," *Orthodoksishe Bletlech,* Warsaw 1923; a Hebrew translation may be found in *Heychal Kotzk*
Weisbrod, David: *Arzey HaLevanon,* Tel Aviv 1945
Yazkan, S. J.: "Perek Mi'Toldot HaChasidut B'Polonia," *Sefer Hayovel Nachum Sokolof,* Warsaw 1904
Zeitlin, Aaron: "Rabbi Mendele Mi'Kotzk," *Hatzofe,* Tishri 5711 (Sept. 9, 1950)
Zeitlin, Aaron: "HaRabbi Mi'Kotzk," *Hadoar,* 5701
Zeitlin, Aaron: "Rabbi Simcha Bunim Mi'Peshischa," *Hadoar,* 4 Tamuz 5705 (1945)
Zeitlin, Hillel, *Hasides,* Warsaw 1925
Zeitlin, Hillel, *Araynfir in Hasides un der Veg fun Habad,* New York 1957

Literature

Cahn, Zvi: *Der Rebbe fun Kotzk,* New York 1950
Opatoshu, Joseph: *In di Polishe Velder*
Opatoshu, Joseph: *Aleyn,* Warsaw 1920
Opatoshu, Joseph: *1863,* Warsaw 1928
Peretz, I. L.: *Di Goldene Keyt*
Stein, M. B.: *Erd in Himel,* Warsaw 1931
Unger, Menashe, *Fun Peshische bis Kotzk,* Buenos Aires 1956

About the Author

Dr. Joseph Fox, scholar, educator, and social worker, can literally be termed a "Perpetual Student."

When he first came here from Opoczno, Congress, Poland, he was more interested in a career as a teacher. After his graduation from Yeshiva University's Teacher's Institute, he devoted the next ten years to being a teacher, principal, and educational director in Harrisburg, Pennsylvania, and Atlanta, Georgia.

While in Atlanta, he studied at John Marshall Law School. He graduated with both a Bachelor's and a Doctorate in Law. His thesis was a comparison between Biblical and Constitutional Law.

Returning to the New York/New Jersey area, he enrolled in the American College for Hospital Administrators. He also accepted a position as Administrator of the Daughters of Israel Home for the Aged in Newark, New Jersey, the largest Jewish institution in the state.

He continued his graduate studies at Yeshiva University and earned a Master of Science in Community Administration. Dr. Fox holds a Doctorate of Philosophy from Dropsie College in Philadelphia.

Dr. Fox has published several books as well as numerous articles in the United States, Canada, and Israel. His book *The Chronically Ill,* published by the Philosophical Library, became a standard text in Hospital Administration.

He also published *The Life and Philosophy of the Rabbi of Kotzk,* in Hebrew, at the prestigious Mossad Harav Kook, Jerusalem, in 1967.

The present volume is the only book in English on this subject. It is a great contribution to Orthodox literature.

———————

Bash Publications wishes to thank the following people for their help in editing *Rabbi Menachem Mendel of Kotzk*: Hallie Cantor, Judy Bendet, Rochelle Miller, Shulamit Goldstein, Annette Bendet, and Avraham M. Goldstein.

ᵀᴴᴱEternal Heritage

A lucid translation of classic and contemporary
traditional sources on the Torah

THE ETERNAL HERITAGE presents to the English reader
access to early and later commentators such as:

- Ramban
- Radak
- Ohr HaChayyim
- R. Bachya
- Kli Yekar
- Chatham Sofer
- Chafetz Chaim
- Maharal
- Vilna Gaon

- R. Simcha Bunem of Pshischa
- R. Levi Yitzchak of Berdichev
- R. Shlomo Kluger
- Divrei Shaul
- R. Yitzchak Zev Soloveichik
- R. Meir Yechiel of Ostrovtsa
- Pardes Yosef
- Chiddushei HaRim
- Meshech Chochmah

**THE ETERNAL HERITAGE gives
access to the English-speaking
public to many Torah commentaries
that until now were available only
in Hebrew.**

By Avraham M. Goldstein

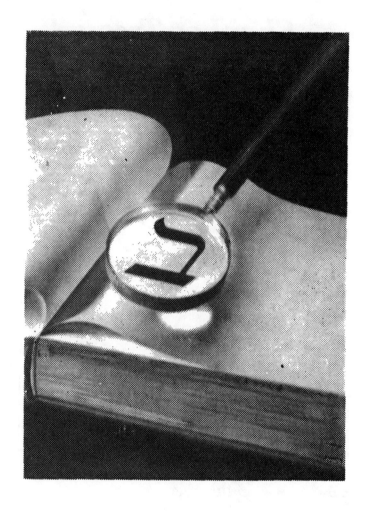

Shabbos Treats
That Grew

A Story by Mayer Bendet

*32 pages 7"x10"
color illustrations
cassette tape*

Shabbos Treats That Grew

Narrated by Simone Bluestein

*Written by Yaffa Leba Gottlieb
Illustrated by Miriam Lando*

Shabbos Treats That Grew is the warm story of a brother and sister who set out to do a small mitzvah, only to find themselves involved in the lives of several Jews in need of their help. Children will delight in this tale, and parents will take pleasure in the character traits that it seeks to promote.